CONNECT OR DIE

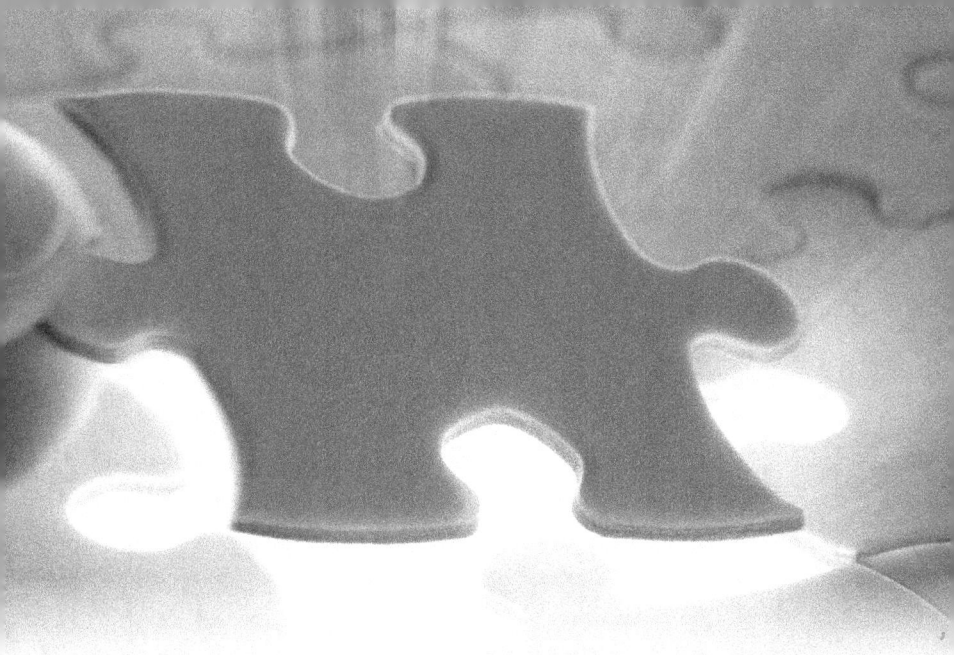

CONNECT OR DIE

BECAUSE YOU HAVE NEVER LIVED UNTIL YOU'VE EXPERIENCED
THE MAGIC OF HUMAN CONNECTION

CHRIS DORRITY
WITH MILLION-SELLING AUTHOR
JOHN MILTON FOGG

Connect or Die: Because You Have Never Lived Until You've Experienced the MAGIC of Human onnection

Copyright © 2019 Chris Dorrity and John Milton Fogg

All rights reserved. No portion of this book may be reproduced mechanically, electronically, or by any other means, including photocopying, without written permission of the publisher. It is illegal to copy this book, post it to a website, or distribute it by any other means without permission from the publisher.

Published by Magic Moments Publishing
Macon, Georgia

Cover and Interior Design by Imagine! Studios
www.ArtsImagine.com

Cover Photo: mikdam/Bigstock.com
Photo on page 99: iStock.com/kupicoo

ISBN: 978-1-7328175-0-0
Library of Congress Control Number: 2019931487

First Printing: January 2019

A man walks on to the empty stage. A big man. (He used to be bigger, 220+ pounds bigger!) There's a hitch in his step—a slight but noticeable limp. One year ago after a car wreck doctors told him he would probably never walk again. He stands there at the very front edge of the stage, scanning the audience, looking down at the front row and up to the folks way in the back of the theater, and stopping to make eye contact with a number of people.

There's been no introduction, and what's really bizarre about this moment is that for the last 15 minutes-plus, the theater has been rockin' out, filled with up-tempo dance music at a volume just a notch or two above too loud.

The high-energy feeling is still in the air, much like after a July thunder storm, but the audience is silent, expectant, even somewhat nervous. Clearly, the abrupt change has some folks feeling a bit uncomfortable.

"You've got a problem," Chris tells them.

He waits. (More unease.) "Everybody does." His soft, southern accent makes him sound like a Georgia preacher. (He was.) "And . . . it's killing you."

A billboard-sized screen in the center of the stage comes to life with the words in bold black-on-white capital letters, CONNECT . . . OR DIE. While the focus of the audience was drawn to that message, Chris has come off the stage and is now down on the floor, and he'll remain there, mostly, walking the two aisles directly connecting with people, one-on-one from one side to the other for the rest of the day.

con·nect
kə'nekt / verb

- To bring together or into contact so that a real or imaginary link is established. "The electrodes were connected to a recording device."

    synonyms: attach, affix, join, fasten, fix, couple, link, secure, hitch, stick, adhere, fuse, pin, screw, bolt, clamp, clip, hook (up); plug (in); add, append.

- To join together so as to provide access and communication. "All the buildings are connected by underground passages."

- To link to a power or other source of supply. "Your house is connected to the main cable TV network."

In the Dorrity Dictionary, the above definition falls short. By a few hundred miles.

"Take *connection* away from any aspect of life and what's left?" Chris asks—and, after a pause, answers, "Nothing. All of life is about *connection*. ALL of life!"

We either *Connect*... *Or Die.*

You most likely want to know Chris's story, unbelievable though it will be to you at times. In his own words will be best. You'll learn some of that soon enough. He tells part of his story at this event.

"Before we begin, I'm going to say something I say at every event I do. I call these 'My Promises.'

"Number 1: I promise I will never lie to you.

"Number 2: I promise I will never ask you to do something that is not for the greatest good of yourself and all concerned.

"There now," he says. "I feel better. Don't you?" In an instant, his laughter fills the theater.

"Okay, in just a moment, I'm going to ask you all an important question. I'm going to ask why you came here today? But before I ask you, I'm going to ask me—and I'll answer myself, too."

With a big smile on his face, Chris asks aloud, "So Chris, why did you come here today?" After a slight pause, he answers.

"I came here today to make each and every one of you feel great about yourself!"

After another pause, where Chris scans the room making eye-contact with as many people as he can, he continues. "That's my job. And it's not just a job. It's my Life Purpose! And I'm going to tell you right up-front how I do that."

Instantly, this graphic appears on the screen behind him.

"Just like the old-fashioned railroad crossing sign," Chris says, "I'm going to STOP everything; all my thoughts and feelings, and focus on you. I'm going to give you my full and complete attention. Who and how you are—right here, right now—will be the single most important thing in my life. And . . . I will LOOK at you.

"Did you see the movie *Avatar*? Remember the Na'vi greeting? Those 10-foot tall, blue-skinned people who gazed directly and deeply into each other's eyes and said, 'I see you.' I'll look at you just like that.

"And I will LISTEN.

"I will listen to you openly, wide-openly without mental-judging, so that I hear both the words and the music. The words of your head and the feeling, the music, of your heart.

"I will CONNECT with each one of you—heart-to-heart—because that's the best way I know that I will have you feeling great about yourself before you leave today."

Chris takes a deep breath and once again scans the entire theater. It seems as if he is making eye-contact with each one of the 1,500 people here. In reality, he probably does.

After a couple of minutes, he begins again.

"Now . . . Why did YOU come here today?" Chris asks, clearly speaking to everybody in the theater. "Talk with me," he says, stretching his arms out, palms up, inviting and encouraging people to interact with him.

A hand goes up from the other side of the room.

Usually in workshops with such a large group of people, there are a number of staff members called "runners" whose job it is to rush quickly to participants who want to speak and hand them a microphone. Chris is his own runner this time.

As he makes his way the long way 'round to the young woman who raised her hand, he repeats his question for everybody, "Why did you come here today? Think about that, please. You all knew the title of the event was *Connect . . . Or Die*, so you came here looking for something from that.

"I'll bet that for most of you, that 'something' you came for was real important. For some of you, it might even be life-or-death important. What is it? What do you want to get from today?"

He reaches the woman who'd raised her hand and politely as always asks her to stand. She is a young girl in her twenties by the look of her. She is wearing jeans and a pale pink sweater. She is slim, slight. Strawberry-blonde and shy.

Chris encourages her to stand and asks her name. She answers, just above a whisper, looking down at her feet while reaching out to take the mic Chris is holding towards her, even though he is still holding it.

"Abby," she says.

"Abby, the lioness," Chris says to the audience and smiles down at her.

Even though she doesn't say anything, the expression on Abby's surprised face asks, "What did you just call me?"

Chris answers her unspoken question. "Abby, the lioness. Just like in Oz," Chris says looking directly at her. "You've got real courage Abby. Did the Wizard give you that, or did you already come here with the courage of a lioness?"

Turning away from Abby, Chris gives his attention to the whole audience, "My friends, every time someone stands and shares today, show them some love. Come on, everybody, give it up for my friend Abby. Abby is a lioness so let's hear you all roar!"

And the audience claps.

But . . .

"STOP! STOP!" Chris exclaims. "Abby, excuse me. Folks, is that the best you can do? Really?

"On a scale of 1 to 10, with 10 being 'Couldn't be better,' and 1 being 'Absolutely pitiful,' how would you rate the applause you all just gave Abby? Shout the number out."

The audience clearly gets the message right away. The highest rating anyone offers is a 6. Mostly 4s and 5s with a good number of 2s and 3s thrown in.

"Look," Chris says, with a more serious tone in his voice that has people paying extra attention. "This conference is not a spectator sport. Only players are allowed beyond this point. Even when you're sitting on the bench and not on the field, you've gotta' be in the game, cheering for your teammates, playing full out! If any of you are not willing or able to bring your best self to this party today, get up now and go get your money back. No harm. No foul. Fair enough?"

Nobody moves.

"Great!" Chris exclaims, "Now, are you up for some training?

"Okay, first thing you do is clap your hands together *harder* or *faster* than the person sitting on either side of you."

A number of people started clapping, but Chris holds up his hand.

"Not yet. I appreciate your enthusiasm, but hold on. I'll tell you when.

"So, you're clear on the instructions? Put your hands together faster, " and he demonstrates, clapping so rapidly his hands are a blur. "Or harder. " Chris slapped his big man's palms together so forcefully they made a popping sound like a ball hitting a bat.

"All right. Ready? Ladies and gentlemen, heeerrreee's Abby..."

The audience, most of whom are smiling and laughing, erupts with loud, vigorous applause.

"Awesome! That's awesome!" Chris exclaims. "Oh, you *are* *awesome!* In fact, you guys are so good, I think you're already for some advanced training.

"So, while you're clapping your hands together harder and faster than the person sitting next to you, I want you to add a shout. You are going to clap your hands and shout as if you have just won a race, won the World Series, won the NBA championship, or won the lottery.

"Okay. Are you ready?" he asks the room now filled with people who are clearly having fun with his first "training."

"Great! So... *Heeerrrreee's Abby*," and the room explodes.

A number of people stand up, and soon the entire audience is giving Abby a standing ovation; everyone is shouting and cheering.

Abby's face is now many more shades pinker than her sweater. As the applause dies down, and people sit down, Chris reaches out and touches her gently on the shoulder. "Tell me," he says, "are you shy, Abby?"

"Oh yes," she says with conviction.

"Well, I hate to break this to you, Abby, but shy people would never raise their hands." Chris laughs along with the audience.

Now, even redder than before, Abby smiles and looks back down at her feet again.

"What's one quality of character a person would have to have to be the very first one to raise her hand in a theater of 1,500 strangers?" Chris asks, sweeping his arm across the room and then turning back to Abby.

"Uh . . . Courage," Abby says, with more question in her tone than answer.

"Yup. Courage." Chris says. "And what is courage?"

"Uh . . . Overcoming your fear," Abby offers tentatively.

"Good one!" Chris exclaims.

"So, Abby, are you fearful? Sometimes? Frequently? Often?" And when she says, "Yes, often," Chris asks the audience, "Anybody else? Any of you fearful, too?"

The theater becomes a sea of raised hands.

"Whoa! I see. So, who would consider this event to be worth its weight in gold to you if you left here being fear*less*?" Chris emphasizes the syllable *less*.

Again, raised hands are all around, including Abby's.

"Great!" Chris says, "*Fearful* means full of fear, right? So, *fearless* would meeaannnn . . . having less fear. Right?"

"Everything you've ever wanted is on the other side of FEAR."

Turning back to Abby, he says, "So, often fear-FULL Abby, when you first raised your hand, you had LESS fear than your normal. Enough *less* so you were willing and able to take that risk and raise your hand. Does that make sense?"

Abby nods, and Chris tells the group, "Fearless doesn't mean you have *no fear*. You're fearless simply by having *less fear* than your usual.

"And being fear-*less*, opens the door to courage."

"So, anybody here FEAR-LESS now?" And as hands went up all around the theater, Chris instructs, "Give yourself a hand!"

Having learned their lesson well, and perhaps wanting to show they had done so, the group demonstrates a robust round of applause.

"This word *courage* is interesting." Chris says. "The root of the word is *cor*—that's Latin for heart. Originally, *courage*, meant speaking or acting from the heart. The Wizard of Oz gave the Tin Man a heart. I think he gave the Lion one, too.

"And speaking of lions . . . " Chris says, turning with a smile to Abby, "So courageous fear-less Lioness, why *did* you come here today?"

Chris is absolutely present, fully focused on Abby's face looking deeply into her eyes—the windows of her soul. Then, he does that remarkable thing that big, male doctors do when they're talking with children. He somehow becomes smaller.

Chris asks softly, "Do you have a problem with *connection?*"

Abby can't help herself. She bursts into tears. "Oh God!" she sobs, shaking her head.

A staff person magically appears with a box of tissues. Chris hands some to Abby, and she wipes her eyes. She starts bringing the tissue up to her nose, but she obviously thinks better of it.

"Go ahead. Blow your nose," he says. She does with a very loud *honk!*

"*Oh my!* A lioness *and* an elephant." Abby and the audience both laugh.

"Give me a hug, girl," he says and opens his arms, but Abby sidesteps him to half-hug off to the side. Chris responds immediately saying "Stop!"

He stands back a bit from Abby and says, "There are no halfway *connections* here. *Connections* happen heart-to-heart. So with every hug you give or receive today—all of you," he says looking up and around the theater, "make sure it's heart-to-heart."

With Abby's discomfort clearly eased, Chris asks again, "Do you have a problem with *connection,* Abby?"

"I do. I mean . . . I must."

"How do you know that?"

"I feel so alone. I always feel alone. Always."

"*She's leaving home after living alone for so many years,*" Chris almost, but not quite, sings the lyrics of the Beatles song. "Like that?"

"Yeah," Abby says with a slight smile. "Just like that."

"Do you feel alone right now?"

"Well . . ." Abby looks around at some of the people sitting close to her. "I mean . . . all these people are here, but I don't *know* anybody. I'm not *connected* with any of them."

"Yet," Chris says.

"Yet," Abby repeats.

"I don't say this to diminish your feelings, Abby," Chris says. "Just to add a bit of context." He is speaking as much to the group as to Abby.

"We're all aware of the 'Opioid Crisis.' It's an epidemic that claims more than 42,000 lives each year. Well, folks, there's a way bigger and badder and more tragic epidemic going in this country and all around the world. It's the 'Loneloid Crisis.'

"Loneliness IS an epidemic, and it's spreading.

"In the past 25 years, the percentage of Americans who have said they were lonely has doubled. It's now 56 percent! That says more than half of all of us feel alone! And we're not just talking old folks. The most affected groups are young adults—Generations X, Y, and Z. The alarming fact is, and I quote, 'Loneliness can kill you.' This is science. Loneliness is like smoking 15 cigarettes a day! That's a fact. Loneliness can take 14 to 16 years *off* your life! That's a fact.

"Another quote: 'Loneliness might be a more significant health factor than obesity, smoking, exercise or nutrition.'

Studies say loneliness increases your risk factor of death between 26 and 60 percent! No wonder suicide rates are at a 30-year high!

"Abby, dear, you ain't all alone in feeling you're alone.

"Ladies and gentlemen, get this, please: CONNECT . . . OR DIE is for real."

After a deep breath, Chris steps back a few feet from Abby and swivels around asking the room, "How many of you feel *connected* with Abby right now?" Hands go up all around the theater. Too many to count, but Chris proffers a guess anyway, "More than half of you. Way more. Isn't that interesting?

"Abby, there are about 700 to 800 people right here right now—people you've never met before, card-carrying strangers who feel *connected* to you in *some* way. How do you suppose *that* happened?"

Chris asks Abby to take her seat for the moment, promising to get back and continue speaking with her very soon, and begins walking around the theater, talking to the entire audience.

"The first definition in the dictionary for *connection* is to bring together, to make contact so that a real or imaginary link is made."

"That's what happened with many of you and Abby. Did any of you *connect* with Abby when she said she felt alone?

Show me your hand if that's true for you, too." A few hundred people raise their arms.

"How about when I asked Abby if she was shy and then told her shy people never raised their hands? Any of you *connect* with her then?" More *shy* hands.

"And when I called her a lioness and told her she had courage... Had any of you had the thought to raise your hand in the beginning when I asked why you came here today, but you held back, and Abby beat you to it? Or you wanted to raise your hand, but... Nah. You didn't want to risk it?" More hands. "And when she burst into tears... Any of you reach out to Abby immediately opening your hearts, *connecting* with empathy and caring for her?" More hands. Many more.

"There are many ways we *connect*. I just pointed out a bunch of ways most of you had some kind of *connection* with Abby. There are about 1500 people who all came together in this room today same time, same place. Does just being here, together *connect* us?

"Turn and look at the person sitting next to you or in front or behind you. Are you *connected* with any of them?" Chris pauses while people looked around.

"How many of you have heard the phrase, 'No man is an island'?"

Chris has been pacing up and down the aisles but he stops now, front row, orchestra center.

"Close your eyes for me, please. I want you to visually imagine you're flying in an airplane sitting in a window seat looking down on the Hawaiian Islands. You're up front in first class, of course. Look down. What do you see?

"There's the 'Big Island' of Hawaii. Then O'ahu, Maui, Kaua'i, Moloka'i. Lana'i. And over there, the two smaller ones (and I always mispronounce these names); Kaholawe and the 'Forbidden Isle,' Ni'ihau. Eight separate, individual islands. Right?

"But if you were a dolphin or maybe a shark and you dove down under the surface of the water what would you see? Are they really separate and apart? Un*connected*?

"Nope. They're all *connected*. Those isolated, individual islands you spot from the air are just the tops and tips of the Hawaiian Alps. Take the ocean away and you'd be looking down at a mountain range like the Rockies in Colorado. Every peak *connected* to one to the other.

"And 'we the people', are just like that. No man or woman is an island, because down below the surface we are all *connected*. When you look deeper than outward appearances, *everything* . . .

"EVERYTHING Is Already, Always, and in All Ways *Connected."*

That's Lesson #1

"Can you see now that *connection* depends solely and wholly on your point of view?" From high up in a plane, those islands are not *connected*. Down below the surface of the ocean, they are *connected*.

"You know the phrase, '*Beauty is in the eye of the beholder. Being connected* or not *connected* . . . Same thing. It's how you see things that counts. That's your world-view. Your *perspective*."

From out of nowhere Chris pulls out a huge pair of green sunglasses with bright yellow lenses, puts them on, and looks around the audience with a big grin. The laughter in the room tells just how silly he looks.

He asks two people across the aisle to stand, has them introduce themselves, and even before they get their names out, the audience explodes with applause.

"Brad," Chris says, "what color is Nancy's blouse?"

"Blue," Brad answers.

"No it's not," Chris said. "It's green." He takes off his oversize sunglasses and hands them to Brad, saying, "Here. Put these on. Now, what color is Nancy's blouse?"

Brad says, "Green."

"My friends, you don't have to be one of *The Color Kittens* to know that mixing blue and yellow makes green. Nancy's blouse is indeed blue, but if the way you see things—your point of view, your perspective—is through yellow glasses, it's green.

"Ladies and gentlemen, we're all always looking out at the world and everybody in it through our own unique perspective."

"I love these lines from the poet Anais Nin. 'We don't see things as they are. We see things as *we* are.'

Chris thanks Brad and Nancy, and as they sit down he says, "What's really important about this is that your perspective is your MINDSET. It's what determines ALL your thoughts, feelings, actions, and interactions in your life and work, at home and in your career. Your perspective controls how you see things and how you see things is the way it—all of *it*—is for you.

"Being separate and set apart, detached, isolated, NOT *connected* . . . That perspective is an illusion. That's not the way life should be, could be and not the way it is.

"I hope I've shown you, even just a little, that our *DIS*connection is NOT the way life really is. Not really reality really.

"Remember the airplane view of the Hawaiian Islands. That's the illusion. Yet as every magician knows, illusions are powerful and persuasive, but once you know how the trick is done, you become a dolphin.

"I don't do politics. Not publicly anyway. I didn't as a preacher. I don't as a teacher and coach. But politics does fascinate me, especially in terms of *connections*.

"Look at the presidential 2016 election and the power of *connection*. What I see happened was the United States was full to bursting with dissatisfied, discouraged, disheartened . . . *DISconnected* voters. So, what happened? The winner won by *connecting* the *DISconnected*.

"How about #MeToo and #TimesUp. Look what's occurred—not just in the U.S., but worldwide: In France it became #BalanceTonPorc (Denounce Your Pig). In Italy, #QuellaVoltaChe (The Time That). And it's happening in England, India, China. All over. And not just in the entertainment business; but also in industry, sports, government, medicine, the media. Everywhere.

"Connecting the DISconnected is the ultimate power-play."

"And I do *LOVE* to play that game. How about y'all?

"Hey, look around this room right now. *Connecting* the *disconnected*. That's what we're all doing here today. We're no fools," Chris says with a laugh.

"What we experience in the world today... The detachment, separation, divorce, isolation, aloneness; all the disengaged, dissociated, disjointed, mixed up stuff around us just ain't real. What God—in whatever way you understand our Creator to be—designed life on Earth to be is all and always *connection*. The idea that you are NOT *connected* in any or every way right here and now is not the truth. Flat out that's flat Earth thinking. It's an illusion. It's a lie! Perhaps the biggest lie of all.

"How many of you..." Chris pauses and takes a slow, deep breath, "have been living that *DISconnected* lie your whole life—up until now? Be honest. Put your hands up if that's you." Most of the people raised their hands. "So, how long have you been doing that? How long ago was it when you first noticed being dis*connected* with the world around you, especially the people around you?

"For most of you, I'm going to guess it was at some age between two and 12? Okay. To be honest, that wasn't a guess. That's a proven scientific fact. Here's the deal: There was a moment—actually, one single incident-instant—back as a child when you made a decision. And what a monumental decision it was! It was literally *life-changing*. You told yourself, 'That's it. I'm done. I am *not* doing *this* anymore.'

"And what you decided was NOT to be your authentic self."

"There's a significant difference in who you are today and the child—your authentic self—you once were. And it's true, 'Unless you come as a small child you cannot enter the kingdom.'

"When was the last time you jumped in a water puddle?" Chris asks. "Let me guess, it's been forever ago. When you were a child—and Mom wasn't looking—you would jump right in stomp an' splash around and have a great time. Now, you walk around it and gripe about the inconvenience.

"When was the last time you danced in the rain? Same as the puddle. But now buy fancy rain boots and an umbrella to avoid getting wet, instead of living in the moment enjoying it.

"When was the last time you told the raw, no-holds-barred truth?"

"I'm talking about telling your mother that dress makes her look fat truth?"

The audience echoes with laughter and chuckles. "By the way," Chris adds with a smile, "I don't suggest you do that!

"You'd learned through painful experience that telling the truth didn't work. That saying or doing what *you* really wanted . . . taking a stand for what you believed . . . being the real you . . . got you into deep poop! You had all the evidence you needed to know that following the crowd, obeying the rules—your parents, the teachers, going along with friends and family—doing what you were told to do, being who and how you were told to be was the ONLY way to stay SAFE, to avoid the pain.

"Literally, our enemy—the Accuser, the Father of Lies—has killed most of our authentic selves, our true spirits. But there's a much bigger truth, 'We were not given a spirit of fear but of power, love and a sound mind.'

Chris has worked his way back to Abby and is standing next to her.

"Does what I've just said make sense?" he asks the room.

"Hi, Lioness," he says, looking down at Abby again. "Want to play some more?"

She says, "Yes," and stands up. A staff person takes her a microphone.

"Abby, you said you were all alone. I think you said 'always.' Is that correct?"

"Yes."

"Besides today, was there a time recently when you had the thought you were alone?"

Abby gazes up at the ceiling looking for the answer. "Yesterday," she replies.

"Good. Now, give me the Twitter version of what happened. A hundred-and-forty characters or less. Just the facts. What happened?"

"I went for a walk in the park on my lunch break."

"Good. And what was the 'alone' thought you had?"

"Well, I looked around at all the people sitting on benches and talking, walking together in twos and threes, a couple holding hands, kids playing with each other . . . And I just felt alone."

"Actually, Abby," Chris says. "There is no feeling called 'alone.' *Alone* is a thought you had."

Lesson #2

Know the Difference Between Your Thoughts and Your Feelings.

"Look and see. Where in your body is that feeling *alone?* Can you locate it? Fear, anger, sadness, gladness . . . those are feelings. But *alone,* that's a thought. Does that make sense to you?"

Abby nods, but she doesn't seem all that convinced.

"You had the thought you were alone, and that thought generated a feeling, perhaps, a bunch of feelings. Thoughts and feelings are *connected,* too. So, when you thought the thought that you were alone, Abby, what did you feel?"

"Empty."

"Really? No feelings at all. That's what empty would be. Nothing. Nothing at all. You didn't feel *anything?*"

"No. I did feel something."

"And . . ."

"I felt sad."

"Because . . . ?"

"I saw all those people together with one and other, and I wasn't *with* anybody. I didn't have anybody to be with. I was all by myself."

"Wild guess. And you *felt* like crying."

Abby, who'd been staring at her feet looked up at Chris immediately. "Yeah, I did."

"Do you feel that way right now?"

With a deep breath, Abby says she does, a little.

"Abby," Chris says, resting his big hand gently on her shoulder, I appreciate and admire your honesty. I know this isn't easy. Thank you, Lioness.

"Folks, I want you to be aware of something here. We'll speak more about this, but for the moment, make a mental note of the difference between *thoughts* and *feelings*. Knowing the difference is important, because it's a *very tough job* to change how you feel. For most of us, feelings rule." Then Chris snaps his fingers while he says,

"But you can change your mind in an instant."

"Want to know the real reason it's so hard to change your feelings?" Chris asks. "This will amaze you. It surely did me.

"I heard about a fascinating project done in Montreal, where neuroscience researchers set about measuring and mapping brain-mind activity. One specific study they did involved the electro-chemical responses participants experienced when they thought about specific words.

"The scientists took all the data they'd accumulated and cross-referenced it looking for similarities, and they found a real mind blower. They were looking for any term that had a close correspondence to the word *change*. And they found one. When they overlaid their brain activity maps on top of each other, there was a near perfect match between the pattern associated with the words *change* and *torture*."

He pauses to let that idea sink in.

"Isn't that incredible!" he says, his eyes wide open big as silver dollars shaking his head in amazement. "Wow! When you or I think about making a change, what comes up for us immediately? Feelings we associate with *torture!* Anxiety. Worry. Fear. Pain. It's no wonder we say people resist change because we do! For good reason.

"Can you see why change–*any and every* change–isn't easy?"

"The feelings associated with the thought are crazy! Give yourself and others a break on that one.

"So Abby, I promise *not* to torture you here. You won't have to *change* anything. I want you to go back in time, say about 10 years ago, I'm guessing you'd be in your earliest 20s. Am I right?"

Abby nods in agreement.

"Bring up a memory of a time back then when you had one of those '*I'm alone*' thoughts and you felt sad, as you did yesterday. Can you remember one of those times?"

Abby identifies a time once in her early 20s when she thought about being alone and felt sad—it was while she was in college and by herself in her dorm room. Chris asks her to reach back even further to another similar experience of alone-thought and sad-feeling from sometime in her teens. She did—the prom date who took somebody else. Then he guides her back into her childhood to an even earlier memory of thinking she was alone and feeling sad. Finally, Chris asks Abby to remember the very earliest time she experienced being alone and sad.

He asks her, "When was that, and what happened?"

Abby was seven or eight. She couldn't remember exactly, but she knew she was in the second grade. She'd raced home as fast as she could from the bus-stop, excitedly bursting through the back door into the kitchen, where her mom was standing at the sink doing the dishes.

In her outstretched hand was a treasure; a paper-maché rainbow unicorn she'd made at school. She felt so proud. It had taken weeks to shape and paint. Abby and her mother shared a love of unicorns.

Abby felt positively triumphant as she extended the gift to her mother, all but shouting, "Mommy, Mommy, look what I made. It's for you!"

She was absolutely unprepared for her mother's reaction.

"Stop it!" Her mother spun around from the sink, her rubber-gloved hands dripping with soapy water. "Can't you see I'm busy. Go to your room this instant, young lady! Right now!"

Little Abby stood frozen—because she was. Although it was a warm spring day, even warmer in the always cozy kitchen, she suddenly felt ice cold. All color had drained from her always pink face. Her pulse and breathing raced. She felt suddenly dizzy and wanted to throw up. Those are all symptoms of shock.

"I said NOW!" her mother yelled, again and turned back to her dishes.

You could have heard a feather drop in the theater.

Abby was standing straight-up like a statue when she'd finished her story. No tears. No expression on her face at all. She is staring straight ahead, hard and cold.

After a long pause, Chris asks,

"That wasn't quite the response you'd expected, was it?"

"No, it wasn't," Abby admits, calmly. Too calmly. Whatever she was feeling inside it was clearly combustible.

"And that wasn't the way your mother normally behaved with you, was it?"

"No, it wasn't," Abby says, again calmly, but the hardness had softened a bit, and the threat of explosion seemed a bit farther off.

"Is there more to the story?" Chris questions. "Had something happened to your mother to cause her to react so unusually, so out-of-character?"

Abby patiently explains that unbeknown to her at the time, her mother had had "the day from hell."

Abby and Tommy lived alone with their mom. Their dad had moved out a few years before, just after her baby brother was born, but they saw him often. He'd stopped by earlier on that day, and he and Abby's mother had a fight. They almost always did.

It was never physical, but always loud and angry. Adding to that, the washing machine had quit working. The electric bill was late, and the power company was threatening to turn off the electricity. Abby's mom had asked her father for more money, and that's what started the fight. They always fought about money.

"So you went to your room?"

"Yes."

"Like a good girl?"

"Of course," Abby replies, and no one misses the sarcasm.

"Abby, I'm going to ask you about the thoughts you had that day and the feelings that came up for you. I want you to do your best to answer me as Abby in the second-grade. As an eight-year-old, not the woman you are today. Do you think you can do that?"

"I'll try."

Chris laughed at her response and asked the audience, "How many of you Star Wars fans remember Master Yoda telling Luke Skywalker, 'Do. Or do not. There is no *try*'?"

Most of the audience raise their hands.

"Well," Chris says, "Yoda was *wrong!* Of course, there is *try.*"

"Would you go into a shoe store, or buy a dress or a sports jacket without *trying* it on to see if it fits? Hey, wanta' *try* these pickled pig's eyes from Borneo? *Noooooo!*

"So, Abby, thanks for *trying* to be an eight-year-old when you answer my questions. I appreciate that." Chris continues, "What's a thought you had . . . The first thought you had when you went into your bedroom. Were you crying even before you got there?"

"I was . . . And I remember telling myself that my mother didn't love me. I mean . . .

"She wouldn't have yelled at me like that if she *really* loved me, and . . . "

Abby doesn't finish the sentence.

"And . . . " Chris prompts.

"And . . . I got suspicious just now that I was about to speak like an adult, not me at eight, but I'll say it anyway." Abby takes a deep breath. "The thought I had was that's why my father left. He wouldn't have left us if he really loved me."

"Too adult, huh?" she asks.

"Maybe. Maybe not." Chris says. "Did you have that thought when you went to your room that day or not?"

"Yeah, I think so," Abby replies. "It wasn't the first time. I'd had that thought a lot."

"Such a lioness," Chris says, shaking his head and smiling at Abby. "And that thought came with what feelings?"

"Sad. So sad." Abby says, clearly composing herself, which is followed by strong sniffle.

"Any other thoughts?"

"Well, yeah." Abby pauses. "This sounds kind of adult, too, but as I remember I was thinking that no matter what I did, it was never good enough. And that also made me sad—and mad."

"Did your mother even *see* the unicorn you made for her, Abby?"

"No. Not then she didn't. I was going to throw it away, but I kept it and showed it to her later that night."

"And she loved it," Chris finishes.

"Yes."

"But you still kept that 'not good enough' thought going?"

"Yeah." Abby looks down, tears welling up in her eyes. "I have it now."

"I understand," Chris comforts and turns to speak to the entire audience.

"I'm going to tell you a story I first learned from a turn of the century author, the last century, the 1900s, named Florence Scovel Shinn. She was an artist and illustrator who became part of what we now call the 'New Thought' movement. In her book, *The Game of Life and How To Play It*, she wrote about the loggers of her day to illustrate an important idea.

"Back then, there were no trucks and highways, so once the lumberjacks had cut down the enormous trees and bucked the branches off to make round logs, they pulled them out of the forest with teams of horses and rolled them into the closest river. Those rivers were the roads they used to transport the logs downstream to the sawmills where they were cut into boards and loaded onto ships and sent out to build the world. Inevitably, these hundreds and hundreds of huge tree trunks would get tangled up in blue. Stuck. They called that a 'logjam.' Not a good thing, because they had to get all those trees flowing downstream.

"Early on, lumberjacks, called 'log rollers,' learned that there was always one tree, which if they pried that one loose, the logjam would break up and all those huge trees would once again start floating down to the sea. They called that one log the 'kingpin.'"

Lesson #3

Pry Loose Your Kingpin

"I'm telling you this story because you and I, each and every one of us, have a kingpin, too. It's that one big fat log in our unconscious that when we pry it loose, our stuck thoughts and feelings loosen up and our energy begins to flow.

"Just as there are hardwoods, such as maple and oak, and softwoods, such as pine and spruce, we have two different kinds of kingpins: Not *enough* and not *good enough*. Sure, everybody has some of each kind, but one is always predominant. But you're *not enough* or *not good enough* for what?

"To LOVE and be LOVED. The most essential *connections* of all. This is our biggest fear. It's why so many of you paid to be here today because of your *not enoughs* and *not good enoughs*.

"You can tell which is yours by asking yourself this question: What do I most consistently want in my life? More, more, more? Or . . . Better, better, better?

"Those of us who answer 'more, more, more,' our kingpin is 'not enough.' Not matter what we do it's never enough. Those of us who answer 'better, better, better,' our kingpin is 'not good enough.' No matter what we do it's never good enough. Look and learn which one fits you best," Chris directs the audience and stands there silently letting the group give that some thought.

"My friends, most people, most of the time—and yes I *am* speaking from my own experience, too—are blind to our own limitations. What stops us. What gets in the way of being who and how we truly want to be in the world. That's why I call the kingpin a blocker. It's something that *blocks* us. Stops us. Prevents us from *connecting*, not only with other people, but most importantly with our true selves."

After about 30 seconds, which is a surprisingly long time when you're sitting there thinking in a theater of 1,500 other silent people, Chris continues.

"When you're aware of your kingpin—your blocker—you have a power tool that helps you identify a place at home or in your career where you're dis*connected*. That blocker is one thing that gets in the way of your *connecting* with people, *connecting* with yourself, and *connecting* with God, your higher power. Once you're able to recognize your blocker, you can choose to do something about it—or not.

"Being *connected* or being *disconnected* are two sides of the same coin."

"Day and night. You can't have one without the other. Each one defines the other. As the Yin and Yang folks say, they're Complementary-Antagonistic Opposites. So, please, don't get caught up in the right/wrong, good/bad, mental judging *thang*.

"You want to *connect* with those things you're in like and in love with, to have more and better *connection* with your aspirations and inspirations, your heart's desires, with every single thing that's for the highest good of yourself and all concerned.

"And you want to dis*connect* with any and everything else that doesn't serve that highest good—for yourself and for others. One most important thing here to know about your kingpin-blocker is . . .

"It's just a habit."

"Because a habit is something you do and have done over and over again without conscious awareness, you start changing a habit, any habit, by being aware you have it in the first place.

Or more accurately in most cases, being aware that the habit *has you!* No matter what I do it's never enough. No matter what I do it's never good enough. Both are simply habits of thought. I like to call them *habitudes*—habits of attitude.

"You can change them. Don't be afraid. This isn't torture." Chris says with a smile.

"You make the change the same way you created the habit to begin with. By simple repetition. Deliberate practice. You'll need to invest the same amount of time and effort in changing a habit as you did in creating it in the first place. Science tells us that will take 66 days, give or take a few minutes." He smiles.

"And by the way, you will *never* get rid of that habit."

"It will always be there with you. How many of you know how to walk? Or drive a car? Or tie your sneakers? Do you think you will *ever* be able to *forget* how to do any of those things—those habits? It just isn't possible for you to forget completely how to walk, drive, or tie shoes. It is the same with any other habit you've developed. You don't forget it. You just replace it with another, newer, hopefully better one."

Suddenly Chris looks down at his watch.

"Whoa!" he said. "I learned as a pastor there's was an 11th commandment. The mind cannot absorb more than the butt can endure. So, let's take a break. What do you think? Lots of people here, so . . . how about we're all back here in 27 minutes, in your seats, and ready to rock an' roll. And, please, we will start on time. Fair enough?"

The up-beat dance music rang out across the room immediately.

Lesson #4

You Are Born a Winner!

In precisely 27 minutes, the music stops, Chris is back on stage and begins speaking, even though about half the audience is still moving down the aisles, and a good number is milling about in the lobby.

"I've never understood," Chris says, "why people start meetings behind time because they're waiting for the latecomers. It's not right to punish those people who kept their commitment to be on time by making them wait for the people who didn't.

"Now, doesn't that make all of you who were in your seats on-time feel *special?*" Chris asks with a laugh.

"Well here's the deal, my *connected* friends . . . *You are special.* Each and every one of you is absolutely unique in all this world. One-of-a-kind. Out of 7.6 billion people on the planet, there's nobody exactly like you. Close, maybe, but like you in every way—no way!

"And I will prove that to you."

"Oh, and while I'm making my case for how special you are, keep in heart and mind that the person sitting next to you, beside you, right in front, seven rows back on the aisle behind you, is special too.

"How cool. One more reason you're all *connected is* because you are all special. Like being in that gifted kids' class in school." Chris laughs.

"So, do you know how you were made? Scientifically speaking, how did you come to become you?

"Reproductive Biology 101. Your father's sperm united with your mother's egg and Walah!' the very beginning of baby you.

"Did you know that the woman's egg is only available to be fertilized for 24 hours? And do you know how many sperm are involved in the process? Take a guess: What do you think?"

A number of people shout out answers.

"I have a million," Chris says and points to the left side of the audience, and like an auctioneer, continues. "Do I hear two million? Who'll give me three million? Four? More?

"Actually my friends, you are far more special that merely one in a million or even one in four million. More, many more. There are somewhere between 300 million and 600 million sperm involved. Each one of you are the result of one—and only one—sperm cell out of hundreds and hundreds of millions that got there first and hooked-up with your mother's single egg, and she produced only one of those eggs each month of her adult life.

"Think of the odds of making that *connection* . . . "

"Now, think of the odds involved in your mother and father ever *connecting* in the first place."

Chris pauses for effect and then says with a laugh, "I have mega-math skills. That's a 1 in 400 trillion chance you would be who you are.

"Use your imagination and trace your family back five or seven generations. Look at all the *connections* that had to be made—grandparents and great, great, great, great, great grandparents, and so on. How many paths magically crossed, random meet-ups, lives that haphazardly came together, all those marriages and births that eventually took place, all of those *connections* down through the generations and hundreds of years that at last resulted in you.

"All those arbitrary, unplanned, indiscriminate, accidental, by chance *connections*. Doesn't that blow your mind? You should be happy all the time—and enthusiastic. Think about it. What if someone would have had one more glass of wine, and you would not have been here? You are so much more than you could ever believe about yourself. You were not owed this life; it is a privilege.

"So now," Chris announces, "let's stand up, and each of you give me a superhero pose."

Immediately Superman's theme music plays as a playful Chris jokingly poses with the audience.

With everyone still standing in their superhero pose, Chris begins telling them, "There is no one even remotely like you. You are unique in all the world. The only one of your kind in the entire Universe. And that makes you special. Very special indeed.

"You *are* nature's greatest miracle."

Chris pulls a paperback book[1] out of his jacket pocket and opens it as he walks down the side-stairs off the stage and starts reading out loud.

"I am nature's greatest miracle," he begins. "Since the beginning of time never has there been another with my mind, my heart, my eyes, my ears, my hands, my hair, my mouth. None that came before, none that live today, and none that come tomorrow can walk and talk and move and think exactly like me. All men are my brothers yet I am different from each. I am a unique creature.

"I am nature's greatest miracle," Chris pauses and looks around the audience before he begins to read again.

"Although I am of the animal kingdom, animal rewards alone will not satisfy me. Within me burns a flame, which has been passed from generations uncounted and its heat is a constant irritation to my spirit to become better than I am, and I will. I will fan this flame of dissatisfaction and proclaim my uniqueness to the world.

"I am nature's greatest miracle.

"None can duplicate my brush strokes, none can make my chisel marks, none can duplicate my handwriting, none can produce my child.

The audience sits entranced by Chris's performance. They seem to be focused on each and every word. He senses that, and their attention fuels him. But drama has given way to something else . . . something . . . spiritual.

---

1 It was *The Greatest Salesman in the World* by Og Mandino

Chris is now speaking totally from his heart, and everybody feels it.

"I am nature's greatest miracle," he says again, but he isn't reading from the book anymore. The book is in his hand down by his side. He is speaking from memory.

"I am rare, and there is value in all rarity; therefore, I am valuable. I am the end product of thousands of years of evolution; therefore, I am better equipped in both mind and body than all the emperors and wise men who preceded me.

"I am nature's greatest miracle," Chris speaks softly, yet powerfully.

"I am not on this earth by chance. I am here for a purpose and that purpose is to grow into a mountain, not to shrink to a grain of sand. Henceforth, will I apply all my efforts to become the highest mountain of all and I will strain my potential until it cries for mercy.

"I am here for a purpose."

Chris stands silently, slowly turning his head from side-to-side searching the audience with his eyes. After a very long, silent minute, he continues "And that single shared purpose for each and every human being who ever has been—or ever will be—born from one sperm and a single egg, is . . . "

Lesson #5

"Our Universal Life Purpose Is . . . To Learn to *Love and Be Loved.*"

"To quote one of my favorite American philosophers, '*The greatest thing that we can do is to help somebody know that they are loved and are capable of loving.*' TV's Mister Rogers said that.

"There's only one way I know you will accomplish learning to love and be loved," Chris exclaims. "*Connect . . . Or Die.*

"What do you say is the #1 *need* you have in your life now?" Chris asks the group. "Just shout it out."

"Love. Acceptance. Security. Recognition." A few people shout, "Money."

"Try this on for size and see if it fits," Chris says.

"The #1 most important need of all is . . . *Relationships.*"

"Remember I said that the universal life purpose for every human being was to love and be loved. And where and when do you experience and express love and being loved?

"In Relationships. To the best of my knowing, there is no other way. The *only* way you can love and be loved is in

Relationship. Relationships are always and in all ways about *giving* and *getting,* and both are required. That's the handshake of God: one hand gives. The other hand gets.

"What happens if you give, give, give, but nobody takes?"

"Think about it: DaVinci paints *The Last Supper* or *The Mona Lisa,* but nobody ever sees them. The Beatles record *Let It Be, Hey Jude, I Wanna' Hold Your Hand,* but not a single person hears any of them. Antoine de Saint-Exupery writes *The Little Prince,* but no one reads it. Giving requires receiving; otherwise, there's no giving. And where does that leave the giver?

"Let me ask ya' something: Does love exist without giving and taking? Give love and nobody gets it—is that really love?

"Of course, we all know people who are always 'on the take' and never give. Takers only. We avoid them like the plague because they carry their disease like rats. They have a contagion that spreads rapidly and kills people.

"Relationships are the place where our greatest joy comes from, a place where appreciation and thankfulness grow wild and free.

"Relationships are the space from where we make a difference in the world, where we contribute and serve each other.

"Relationships are where we build bridges over troubled waters where empathy and compassion glow in the dark.

"Relationships, Friendships, Partnerships, Leadership. These are the places where life comes alive, where our lives are lived.

"God said, 'It is not good for man to be alone,' and he wasn't just talking about Eve. A life lived alone is a death sentence. I live by the philosophy that no one can do life alone.

"My friend and mentor John Fogg—and something I highly recommend is that you make it mandatory that your friends be your mentors, too—calls this 'Shipping & Receiving.'

"Relation*shipping*, Friend*shipping*, Partner*shipping* and Leader*shipping* are what life is all about. John says that when you do that *shipping* business really well, you *receive* all the rich rewards life offers. And all that *shipping* is all *connection*. In fact, *Relationship* (and Friendship, and Partnership, and Leadership) and *connection* go beyond being simply synonyms. They are two different looking and sounding words that mean the *exact same thing!*

"Look at your life at home and in your career . . . do you think that's true?

"Ever heard the saying, 'It's not what you know, it's *who* you know?' Do you think that's true?"

Lesson #6

"When I Say 'CONNECT . . . OR DIE,' I'm Not Kidding."

"When we are not *connected* in healthy, happy, heavenly, Relationship with other people, with ourselves, and with the God of our understanding, we are dead. We may be 'dead man walking,' but dead we are. Stone. Cold. Dead.

"And don't forget," Chris adds with a Shakespearean flourish, '*To connect or not to connect. That is the question.*'

While Chris has been speaking about Relationships, he's been working his way around the room ending back up front in the center.

"Okay, I'm going to ask you all to do something with me now, but I have a few instructions to give you first.

"I'm going to ask a few of you to volunteer to speak with me one-on-one. I'll ask each one of you I speak with a couple of questions. Just be honest with me, please. I promise you will be safe, and you'll get no mental judging from me.

"I want to learn what you think and feel about some of the things we've talked about today. And please . . . PLEASE (he emphasized the word), tell me the truth, the whole truth and nothing but the truth."

"Let's practice the skill of authenticity."

"So, who's willing and able to play?"

Chris makes his way to a man who has raised his hand about halfway back. One of the runners has come down from the rear of the theater and is there already with a hand-held microphone, which he gave to the man who was standing when Chris got there.

Chris sticks out his hand. "Hi, I'm Chris. What's your name?"

"George," the man says with the mic too far away from his mouth to be heard.

Chris reaches out and gently raises the man's hand so the mic was closer. "Try that," he says. "What's your name again?"

"George," the man repeats, but this time he is loud and clear.

"Folks," Chris says, "please show George the same love you did for Abby earlier. Come on, baby and give him some love with your applause."

The entire group gives George an explosive round of applause, with most people standing and cheering.

When the laughter and chatter die down, which takes a good while, Chris says to George, "Tell me George, how did that appreciation make you feel?"

"Wow," George says. "That was really something."

"Happens to you everywhere you go, right, George?"

"Hardly." George laughs.

"Folks, I'm sure you're aware of the positive effect your applause had on Abby and George, but I want you to notice the impact it had *on you*.

"Motion creates emotion."

"Normally we assume that when we're applauding for people like you just did, we're giving *them* something. Remember what I said about *giving* and *getting*. What did you *get* by *giving* that fantastic applause to George?"

"Remember earlier when I spoke with Abby and told her she could change her mind in an instant? Well this is the number one way! Motions change our emotions. It will make dead men come to life.

"Emotion. Feeling. Energy. *Chi* in China. *Ki* in Japan. *Prana* in India. *Nafs* and *Ruh* in Islamic countries. Here in the West we call it *Spirit*. It is what God breathed into Adam that brought human kind to life.

"That's what you just did. You all just breathed life into this room.

"Anybody feel more *energized* and *alive* now than before? More engaged? More all present and accounted for? Happier?

"More *connected* . . . ?"

"Interesting isn't it?" Chris muses and turns back to George.

"So, George, if you've recovered from your recent rock star treatment, I have a question for you. I'm just curious, besides that applause, what's one of the best things you've learned about today?"

George is clearly thinking before speaking. After a pause he says, "That no man is an island. That we're all—as you said—already and always *connected* with each other. Like the mountains."

"And what makes that idea important for you George?" Chris asks him.

"Well . . . " Thoughtful George is thinking again. "I realized that whenever I experience being dis*connected,* that's on me. That's not the way it really is, so if I'm not feeling—or thinking—I'm *connected,* that's *my* point of view. My perspective, you said. And I can change that. It's a choice I have."

Chris puts his hands to each side of George's upper arms, moves him aside, and sits straight down in George's empty seat.

He stays there for a few quick moments looking up at George with a big smile.

"Tell you what, George. That was so good—really *so good* that I want you to teach the rest of this program today."

The audience laughs, as does George, although he does so with some obvious embarrassment.

Chris stands back up and takes George's hand, shaking it and saying, "George, that was awesome! Absolutely. You were awesome. You *are awesome*. Thank you. Give me a heart-to-heart *connection* hug."

"Heart-to-heart," George repeats

"Good man," Chris laughs. "Give George another hand.

"Who's next?" Chris calls to the audience when their applause quiets. "I know George is a hard act to follow, but not to worry. Just be the real you. What's one of the best things you've gotten from today?

"And look, while the rest of you are sitting there listening to each of these people, I have an assignment for you. I'll explain more later, but for now, what I'm asking you to do is to *LISTEN* in a very specific way. I want you to *listen FOR* the *values* of the person who is speaking."

Lesson #7

"Our V*alues* Are Those Things That Are Most Important In Our Lives. They C*onnect Us*."

"Values are always what's at the heart-of-the-matter especially when something is the matter with someone, something upsetting, something that's not right.

"What makes *values* so important for us here today is that people *connect* with each other at the level of *values*. Our shared *values* are what *connect* us.

"Have you ever noticed that soccer moms hang out with other soccer moms? Business people speak easily and enjoyably with other business people. Dancers with dancers. Jews with Jews. Vegetarians with vegetarians. The reason all those people relate so well with each other, that they get along so quickly and easily, is they're *connecting* with each other's *values*.

"I know social scientists say that what connects us is *shared activity*, but I believe it's the *values* we experience and express from engaging in those specific activities that really attracts us to each other.

"Soccer moms—no matter how different their ages, or races, or education, or anything else—share *values* with each other, such as sacrificing for their kids, wanting them to have fun, to learn to play together, get the benefits of physical exercise, healthy competition, learning to be part of a team.

"*Values* are the essence of what connects us in all our Relationships, Friendships and Partnerships.

"I believe our *values* are spiritual, because *values* live in our hearts, and the heart is spiritual."

"You'll hear people speak about their *values* when I ask the second question: What makes such and such important, or special, or something you appreciate? That's a right-brain question. A heart question. You can't answer it with your left brain, with your head.

"More to say about that head-heart business, too. Just trust it for now.

"So, listen FOR people's *values* when I'm speaking with them. And as you do, notice how knowing that person's values *connects* you with him or her."

Chris speaks with two more people. Each is greeted with great applause when they stand up and a big heart-to-heart *connection* hug from Chris.

He asks each person what is one of the best things they learned, or appreciated most, about what he or she has experienced at the event so far. He follows each of their answers with his second question, asking what it was that made that important, interesting . . . or special or something they appreciated so much.

"Now, it's your turn," Chris announces to the group.

"Beth and Alex, I've demonstrated the conversation with George, so you should know how it goes. Just two simple questions.

"Question 1. What's one of the best things you've learned from today so far? And then, Question 2: What makes that—the thing the person said he or she has learned—'important for you?' You can use other words in that second question, like special, interesting, useful, valuable, something you appreciate. Just feel it out and go with the word which is best.

"Now, the #1 skill you're going to need to do this exercise successfully is . . . ?" And he pauses for an answer.

Lesson #8

"Listen. Listen. And Listen for Values."

"Absolutely! Great answer. And what specific kind of listening?" Chris asks.

There was a pause, and then someone yells, "For values."

"That's a gold star," Chris yells back. "Come see me after, and I'll give you a signed copy of my book. Excellent!

"So, pick a partner. It is best if it's someone you didn't know before you came here today. You're welcome to move around; actually I encourage that. So, pick a partner. Say, "Hi," tell them your name, and give him or her a heart-to-heart *connection* hug. I encourage that, too.

"One of you go first and ask the other about the 'best thing,' and I'll let you know when three minutes are up, and you can switch who's asking and answering.

"Okay, start now. Grab your partner. Do-zee-do.

"Don't waste time trying to *find* the right somebody. In this case, Yoda *was* right. Don't *try,* just grab somebody, anybody. You want to be asking and answering as soon as possible," Chris instructs.

A theater of 1,500 people speaking with each other is not a sound you hear every day. Although not all that loud, it is commanding, like a hard, steady rain or a monastery full of resonant Gregorian chanting.

At the three-minute mark, Chris asks them to stop and give the other person his or her turn to answer.

In three more minutes, Chris, who has moved to stand up on stage, says, "Stop there, please. So, how'd ya' do? Did any of you make a *connection* with someone new?"

If there were people who didn't raise their hands, it is hard to find them.

"Great!" Chris beams. "So, there were about 750 Relationships that were started. Any Friendships? Anybody fall 'in-like' with each other?"

More than a few hands are raised. Lots more than a few.

"So, how'd that happen? What did you do that *connected* the two of you together in Relationship and the beginnings of Friendship?"

So many people speak at once it is nearly impossible to pick out a clear answer. Chris says, "Hold on. Raise your hand and let me pick somebody." He chooses a woman in the front row.

She stands up and says her name is Katya. As the audience bursts into enthusiastic clapping and hooting, she turns and accepts their applause with an exaggerated, flourishing curtsey. The audience is delighted and shows it with even louder applause, cat calls and a number of shouts of "Bravo! Brava!"

"Katya, will you come up here and join me?" Chris asks through his broad smile. "I'm guessing you've been on stage before."

While no one has been paying much attention, two comfortable looking chairs have been placed on stage. Between them is a low table with a big bunch of colorful, fresh-cut flowers and a couple of bottles of spring water on it.

Katya goes up on stage, guided by a staff member. Chris greets her with a hug, and, holding her hand with both of his, he steers her towards her chair.

"So, dear lady," he begins, "do you remember what your answer was to my question of what you did that *connected* the two of you together?"

"Of course," she says, with a hard to locate accent that was somewhat smoky and definitely mysterious. "We spoke together."

"You had a conversation," Chris offers.

"Yes," Katya says. "We had conversation."

"I want to speak more about that Katya, but I'm just so curious to learn where you're from. Your accent is charming, and actually . . . " Chris interrupts himself with a laugh. "You sound like a Russian spy."

Katya breaks up immediately returning his laughter, shaking her head and shyly covering her mouth with her hand. She quickly composes herself and says, "I am Czech—born in

Czechia, the Czech Republic—but my family is Russian. From Siberia," which she pronounces *See-beer*. "But I am gypsy, not a spy."

"You didn't sound like you were from Georgia," Chris says, enunciating *Georgia* with an even more pronounced Southern accent than his normal.

They both laugh. "I do live in Georgia. Atlanta," Katya volunteers.

"You're the first Georgia gypsy from Czechoslovakia I've ever met."

"Folks," Chris interrupts his conversation, "your assignment right now is to . . . " He lets his sentence hang in the air as he waits for the group to answer.

"Listen," the audience loudly fills in the blank.

"For . . . ?" Chris asks.

"Values," they reply.

"I swear. Y'all are *the* smartest group of folks I have ever met in my life." Chris smiles and turns back to focus on Katya.

"What do you like best about living in Atlanta?" Chris asks.

"Everything but summer," she says. "I call it 'Hot-lanta.' Too hot, but only a few months."

"I know Atlanta in summer. *HOT-lanta* is right! If I go to a meeting in July or August, even first thing in the morning, I take two shirts, because my first one will be soaking wet just walking from the parking lot.

"So what's one part of 'everything' that you like about living in Atlanta, Katya?"

"It's so green, like living in a forest. I grew up in a city: many buildings, apartments, streets, sidewalks. Not trees and grass and gardens."

"What do you like most about all those trees and gardens?"

"Nature. I take deep breaths and feel very alive with nature. Healthy. It makes me happy.

I also like the Piedmont Park, the Lake Clara, the trees. There is playground and picnic places—and tennis courts. So beautiful, and peaceful and fun. We walk there from my house."

"You a tennis player?"

"I am a Czech!" Katya declares, as if she is surprised Chris had asked her.

"Ah yes," he says. "Two Martinis and an Ivan."

"Yes!" Katya exclaims. "You know tennis?"

"I do," Chris tells her. "We all play. My daughter Reagan is competing now. Of course, I know Martina Navratilova. She's the greatest female player of all time. And Martina Hingis—even though she played for Switzerland—and Ivan Lendl. So, you play."

"I do," Katya says.

"Any good?"

"Yes," Katya says, and there is no doubt in anybody's mind that she is.

"What do you like best about playing tennis?" Chris asks.

**"I'm good. I like being good.
I like to win."**

"I am with you there Katya. I *love* to win. Do you hate to lose?"

"No," she says matter-of-factly. "I don't like it, but hate . . . I don't like 'hate'. There was enough of that as a child. You don't win tennis always. Win and lose. It's the game."

"I love your attitude, Katya. I'm curious, how do you feel when you lose?"

"It's okay," she says. "Winning is more fun. But losing learns more. And I like lessons more than playing now. They're faster. I do more. In games, there's always much standing still waiting."

"You mentioned 'playground' when you spoke about the park. Do you have kids?"

"Two."

"How old?" Chris asks.

"Olga is 18. Alexi—Alexander—is 15."

"Oh my!" Chris exclaims. "You don't look anywhere near old enough to have such grown up children."

"Katya smiled and nodded her head. "I am 47."

"Like I said . . . I would have guessed in your 30s. Good for you."

"I like to be healthy," Katya says.

"You look like you do," Chris replies.

Chris holds up his hand like a stop sign and speaks to the audience. "Are you with us? Don't you think this woman is a treasure? I am so curious about Katya. I'm like a prospector digging for gold, and asking questions and listening to her answers are my pick and shovel." He turns back to Katya.

"How did you come to the United States?"
"I followed my husband."
"What brought him to the America?"
"He is American. We met in Prague."
"Love at first sight?"

"No . . . Well for him, yes," Katya laughs.

"For me, it was like at first sight."
"How did you meet?"
"He was friends with my friends. He was going back to America from Berlin. He stopped in Prague, and they were to have dinner together and invited me to meet him. They thought we would like each other."
"And you did . . . "
"And we did," Katya says, adding, "very much. He was fun."
"You said you followed him to America. What happened?"
"After that dinner, we spoke often on the telephone. Soon, he was calling me every night. That was 1997 and 1998. The phone was expensive. One night he told me his phone bill was $1,600. He couldn't afford to talk to me living in Prague. So he asked me to come to America. To Atlanta."

"And you did. Wow! That was brave."

"Abby," Chris calls out. "She's your sister from another mister. Another lioness."

Katya laughs. "We met in Prague sometimes. He traveled to do business in Germany and Paris. He worked for Mr. Ted Turner. CNN International. He stopped to see me, and I fell in love with him, so it was easy.

"And those days, life in the former Soviet Union countries was not good. Hard for everybody. We all wanted to go to America. It was a chance for me. I took it."

"Still, a brave move," Chris says.

Katya smiles. "I was music teacher, but I no longer had my job. He told me—he is Anthony—Tony—that he would help me find a place to live and work. So. Easy. When I came to America, he met me at the Airport and asked me to marry him."

"Right there? In baggage claim?"

"Yes. In baggage claim."

"Did he get down on one knee?"

"Yes. Down on his knee."

Katya is smiling.
Chris is smiling.
Everybody is smiling.

"What a wonderful story. An *amazing* story. And you are amazing and wonderful. Absolutely." Chris says to Katya, and turning to the audience he says, "Folks, that's how it goes. We be *connected*. What did that take—five minutes, maybe five and a half? And if we both had the time, made the time, it could have gone on lots longer.

"Don't you want to know more about her? I sure do.

"Like what makes Katya say she's a gypsy—remember that: 'I'm not a spy. I'm a gypsy'? And that bit about not hating losing. She said she had enough of *that* as a child. Tell me more! And her kids, I don't know anything about her kids. I have kids. How are Katya's like mine, and how are they different? Tell me more! What does her husband do? She said he worked for Ted Turner. Tell me more! A music teacher. Tell me more! Growing up in Soviet times. Tell me more! Czech. Tell me more!

"Tell me more! Tell me more! Tell me more!"

"Fascinating. The woman is a gold mine, as I said. Special. We all are. We just need to *connect*. Not like friends on Facebook. That's 'relationships-lite.' Not drive-by postings: 'Awesome. Cool. You rock!' Really *connect* with each other.

"Katya," Chris asks, "Do you like me?"

She blushes and says yes, she does.

"I like you, too. A lot."

"Folks, what do you think made Katya like me? How did we fall in-like with each other?"

He lets his question hang in the air a little, then continues. "We *connected* when we said 'Hi' to each other. That's all it takes. We deepened that *connection* because I was interested in her favorite subject. I was curious about who and how Katya is and was as a person.

"Katya, did you feel good about our conversation?"

"Yes. It was fun for me."

"My friends, is fun one of Katya's values? You bet. *Fun* in the park. Her husband was *fun*—one reason she fell in love with him I'll bet. Yes?" He asks looking at Katya, and she nods.

"Our conversation was *fun*."

"The number one skill you need to become a Master *Connector* is simple curiosity. Be curious about who and how the other person is. Be interested. Be *fascinated*. So how do you do that?"

Chris answers his own question, "It's a conversation."

Lesson #9

Connection Is Created In Conversation.

"And since everything we do and be is about *connection* . . .

"Life is created in conversation."

Chris stands up. "How is *connection* created?" He asks the audience.

"Conversation," comes the unanimous response.

"Absolutely!

"Now, it's time for the lunch break. A working lunch. Your assignment is to hook up with someone and have a '*Conversation For Connection*,' just like I did here with Katya. Be a miner

49er, prospecting for gold. Your pick and shovel are asking questions and listening.

"A great way to begin is simply ask your partner 'Where do you live?' Then ask, 'What do you like best about living there?' Be curious. Interested. Go for the gold. Learn all about him or her. *Ask questions and* . . . Listen. Listen. Listen.

"Tony Robbins has a quote I love:

> **"Ask lousy questions, get lousy answers.**
>
> **Ask great questions, get great answers."**

"So, what will you do over lunch . . . ?"

Dozens of people yell out, "Ask great questions."

A broadly smiling Chris then asks the group if anybody has any questions or concerns about their lunch assignment. There are none.

He tells them the break will be 97 minutes, smiles, and encourages them to be back on time.

He explains that the support team had maps of the closest and quickest places to eat. Then, before he sends them on their way, he asks Katya to stand and says, "Folks, show Katya how much you liked her and how *connected* you all are with her."

He receives the most enthusiastic applause of the day.

"Have fun!" Chris shouts above the clamor and the now expected dance-party music, waves to the group and turns to Katya giving her a big heart-to-heart bear hug.

Remarkably, there isn't one person who wasn't settled in their places when Chris walks back out on stage, although many people don't sit down until the music stops.

"Good job!" He says. "Thanks for being on time. Thanks for keeping your commitment—to me, to each other. To yourself. And thanks for keeping your word.

"Give yourselves a great big hand!" The entire audience jumps to their feet smiling, clapping, chattering away, cheering, and whistling. It is great!

Lesson #10

How You Do Anything Is How You Do Everything. So Play Full Out!

"Something I'm asking you to remember is that being on time isn't a value. It's an experience and expression of a number of values a person has.

"I mentioned commitment, and integrity, which is what keeping you word is all about. Being on time is something people who are considerate of others do. People who care show up on time. They are people we know we can depend on. I'll bet you can come up with even more on-time values. Oh . . . And does your, my, our, being on time have anything to do with being *connected* with each other?"

Chris let them think on that question for a quick bit. Then he says, "Speaking of values and *connection,* how was lunch? How'd your assignment go? Raise your hand and talk to me."

Many, *many,* more people are raising their hands than did in the morning session. Chris comes down off the stage and speaks with at least six or seven people.

After he asks each person's name, and they receive their rousing applause, Chris asks, "What was the best thing about your lunch conversation?" And then he asks each one, "What made that best thing important or special or so enjoyable for you?"

Every single person is lit up, enthusiastic, and excited. When Chris finishes with one person, others in the audience are pumping their hands up and down, straining to be recognized like little kids who know the answer to the teacher's question.

It is great fun to watch. Even more fun to be a part of. The energy in the room is remarkable, so Chris remarks on it. "My friends, can you feel the energy in this room right now? Pretty amazing, doncha' think?

"I'm going to let you in on a secret . . .

"It's all about *the energy.*"

"All and always and in all ways. Everything is energy, especially when it comes to *connecting.*

"Motion creates emotion. That principle is not just true for taking physical action. It works with our taking mental action, too.

"I want you to do something with me now. I hadn't planned on doing this, but you guys are just so great, I've gotta' do it.

"Before I do, let me ask: How many of you have read the books, been to the workshops and seminars, or even had coaching and counseling, so that now you never-ever allow a negative thought to enter your mind?"

A good many people, probably a few dozen, raise their hands.

"So, you've taken as gospel the wonderful title of Peter McWilliams classic self-help book, *You Can't Afford the Luxury of a Negative Thought,* yes?

"McWilliams said that his negativity problem wasn't that he saw the glass as half-empty, instead of half-full. His was more serious than that. When he looked at the glass, he was sure someone was going to steal it, or at minimum knock it over and spill it all out.

"So, for those of you who can't afford the luxury, I'm asking you to suspend that idea for a brief moment here today, so you can fully experience what I want you to learn. Are you guys willing and able to do that? It's safe. I promise. I'll make sure of that. Will you do that for me, for yourself?

"Anybody not willing and able to do that?" Because no hands went up, Chris continues.

"Great, now, first thing. I want you to take the pulse of your energy right here and now, and give it a rating from one to 10. I'm asking you to gauge how you *feel* with 10 being *couldn't be better,* and 1 being *absolutely awful.* You're darn near flat-lining. Dead.

"Got that? Take your pulse, rate your energy level, right now—one to 10. Raise your hand when you've done that."

When it seems just about every hand is raised, Chris continues.

"I have a question for you. When I ask it, think about it. Really *think* about it. And let any feelings you have associated with it come right up. Okay? Here's the question:

"What's the worst thing that's happened to you in the last five years?"

Chris pauses for a few seconds and then adds, "And what made that experience so bad?"

He gives them time to consider their answers. Not long. Maybe 15 seconds or so.

"Okay, stop," Chris instructs. "Take your pulse again. Rate your energy as of this very moment on a scale of one to 10, just like you did before.

"Now was your rating the same as before I asked that 'worst thing' question, higher, or lower? Shout it out: higher, lower, or the same."

The unanimous response is lower.

"Lower. On a scale of one to 10, how many points lower?"

The answers range from two to four points lower.

"Great. Thanks. I want you to know that this demonstration has been done all around the world, from people and cultures as diverse as Iceland, India, and Iran to Thailand, Trinidad, and Texas. Your result was the same as all theirs: lower by two to four points.

"Now, I will *not* leave you down there. Here's the next question . . .

"What's one of the best things that's happened to you this week?"

Chris pauses a few seconds and then asks, "And what made that so good? What made that special for you?"

After 10 or 12 seconds, he asks again, "Rate your energy right now as of this moment on a scale of one to 10, just like you did before."

He gives them a little time and then asks, "Shout it out: higher, lower, or the same as after you answered that worst thing question?"

The response is unanimously higher.

"Back up again, the same as when we first began this exercise. Or even higher than when you started?"

The responses are mostly the same with many higher.

"That's great! Give yourself a big hand for playing full out with this." And they did. Everybody had that one down now.

"What this demonstration illustrates is a very simple, not-so-secret secret." Chris explained. "Focusing your attention on what's wrong sucks your energy. Putting your awareness on what's right grows your energy. Builds your energy up, up and even away!

"And here's what's most important," Chris says.

"What you focus on becomes the center of your life."

"Do you know anybody who always talks about their problems, about what's wrong? Negative, negative, negative. How do you feel when you're with them?

"Now there's a person, place, and thing you want to *DISconnect* with!

"And, man, do we live in a world focused on what's wrong. I say that's one huge reason our world is so *disconnected*.

"Ever wondered why so many people—and you may be one yourself—are so tired all the time? Now, you know why. They've had the energy draining out of them by focusing on all their problems, on what's wrong, for so long they're just plain exhausted.

"Want to blow your mind in a good way? Ignore the negative news for one week. Try it. Just one week. You can do that!

"Turn off the TV. Forget your news feed. Pay zero attention to Facebook and Twitter. Really. Just try it. You won't die, I promise. Just for seven days.

"Go on a negativity diet. Don't eat anything *wrong* for a week."

"Any of you carrying the weight of the world on your back? You guys will lose a few hundred pounds on the negativity diet.

"Remember what you focus on becomes the center of your life. What do you suppose your life will be like when you're focused on—*CONNECTED* to—what's right, what's good and great about life? When you're so busy looking for value you don't see the faults?

"Do you imagine you might be happier? Healthier? More at home in the world? Have more peace. More joy. More fun?

"Katya, did you hear that? More fun!" Chris laughs along with the group.

"And you will have more ENERGY, I promise."

Chris pauses and then says, "And . . . will you be more *connected?*

"I listened to a podcast recently where author John Eldgridge introduced a concept I'd never heard of before: 'Micro Practice.'

"One big problem with so many of the instructions we get from self-help teachers and the church, no matter how beneficial they'd be for us to do, is that they're so complicated and time-consuming we just won't do them. And because they are they aren't useful. Have you been there?

"So a 'micro practice' is a mini-exercise, a quickie, some something that's really short and sweet, but still gets positive results. Here's one of mine. I want you to try this for one week.

"You can commit to doing this for 7 days because it's easy and fun."

"Three times each day ask somebody—anybody, family, friends, co-workers, a clerk in a store, the cop on the corner, a stranger, anybody. Just ask, 'What's the best thing that's happened to you this week?' Then listen, really listen intently to the person's answer.

"Then ask question number 2: 'What made that so special?' Or interesting, useful, important, something you appreciate—choose the word that's most appropriate.

"Simple. Yes?" Chris asked. "Three times each day for one week. Will you do that?

"And if you're up for it, if you're willing and able to max it out, make that five times a day.

"It's a great way to quickly *connect* with people. And," Chris adds, "you just might find that it's a great way to *connect* and *re-connect* with yourself in a positive, energy-building way.

"Now' you're all sitting down. That's good because if you were standing up what I'm about to say just might make some of you fall down.

"All this *disconnectedness,* aloneness, separation, isolation . . . Your preoccupation with your problems and what's wrong . . . All that negative, negative, negativity . . . All of that . . .

"Is not your fault."

"Wait! What? What did he say? It's not my fault?" Chris says.

"That's what I said.

"Let me guess: Most of you are self-improvement, personal growth and development junkies," Chris adds with a laugh. "Yes?

"As I pointed out before, you've read the books, listened to the CDs and podcasts, and watched the TED Talks on YouTube. Am I right? So, most of you are you are pros at all of that stuff. This isn't your first self-help rodeo.

"So, if that bit about 'It's not your fault' didn't knock you over, I bet this one will.

"You're a victim."

"Wait! What? Did he *really* say that? Did Chris Dorrity just tell me *I am a victim?*

"Yes, Chris Dorrity—that's me, by the way—just said something every other self-development, self-help guru, psychologist and psychiatrist, spiritual teacher, preacher, author, and speaker has always said you're not. You are a victim.

"How do ya' like them apples?" he said with a big laugh. "You're a victim, and it's not your fault."

He waits for a bit and then says, "So, anybody want me to explain *that* one?"

The theater is a sea of raised hands.

He smiles. "Thought might get your attention.

"Anybody here have kids?" Chris asks. Lots of hands.

"Anybody have parents?" Laughter and more hands.

"Okay, how many of you who have children, and how many of you who had a mother and father, or even just one or the other, or an aunt or grandma who brought you up . . . How many of those people went to Parent School?"

Not a hand was raised.

"Isn't that amazing!?! Probably THE most important job on the planet, but nobody went to school to learn how to do it.

"Folks, each and every one of us here, there, and everywhere today is a victim of how we were brought up—or *brung up*," Chris says with a smile.

"Even those of us who grew up with loving, wise and caring parents, nuclear families, indoor toilets, lace curtains, two cars and three TVs. We imitated our parents, copied their behavior, designed our personalities, said and did what worked, what kept us safe, even if we had to fake it to make it, in order to win their love and get their attention.

"Abby," Chris calls out, "what do you think? Any of that ring true for you?"

Abby nods and says that it did.

"You know it's not your fault, right? I mean, you had your little bottom handed to you on a hot plate because you gave your mom a rainbow colored unicorn as a gift. *Come on* . . . .

"What did you do wrong? Nothing! *No thing!*

"Which is why I say you're a victim. Falsely accused and made to feel ashamed. Convicted of a crime you didn't commit. An innocent *victim*.

"Anybody else getting this? Any of you relate? Resonate?"

"So this bit about being a victim rings true for most of you?"

Most of the audience nods that it did. Some seem confused. Almost all are quietly thoughtful. If you have taken the pulse of the energy in the room, you'd have noticed it has dropped considerably. Chris notices.

"All right. Everybody up! Stand up, please right now. Up! Up!" Chris instructs.

"It's party time!" he announces. "Jump up up on your feet and let's start moving!"

"The energy in this room is draining like a downspout in a rain storm. Let's ramp and amp it up. Now!"

Right on cue, the theater fills with the commanding sounds of a Zumba class in high gear. This goes one better than the previous dance-party music.

You could feel the addictive bass beat through the floor. You didn't need to speak Spanish to be carried up and away by the rhythmic repetitious lyrics. And you'd have had to be at death's door not to start moving your feet and hips instantly.

Up on stage leading the way is Chris, nearly all 300 pounds and 6' 4" pro football lineman of him cutting moves like a Latin teenager. The aisles quickly fill with dancers, and there are more than a few silver-haired folks dancing right along with them.

Chris has quickly come down off the stage and is dancing with three people from the front row.

He lets the song play out, and starts speaking at the same time he is getting his breath back.

"Aw right! How you all feelin' now?"

Chris asks, a bit breathless, but beaming.

He bends over, hands on his thighs, and then stands back up quickly. "Whew! Spent some time as a youth pastor," he says. "But it's been a few years. Out of practice. Mama!"

People are back in their seats when Chris says, "Motion creates emotion. Do you think we're on to achieving something here?"

"Anytime things get heavy, or you sense the energy draining, just play that music. Keep it on your iPhone. Works every time. Guess that's one of those *micro practices* they were talkin' about.

"Okay, Abby dear, I've got a question for you."

Abby stands up. Chris stays at the front of the room and a runner takes Abby a microphone.

Once she has the mic in hand, Chris asks, "Abby, remember I said that there's an instant when we make a decision as a child that's life-changing? It's a moment where we set aside our authentic self and put on a personality that I call the *false self*. It keeps us safe, helps us navigate the stormy seas of life. You remember?"

"I do," she says.

"Try this on for size and see if it fits.

"Now, remember, this isn't what you told yourself as a seven- or eight-year-old. I'm using adult vocabulary now. Did you decide that the way to get along with your mom, the way to be with her so you didn't get hurt like that again, was to become a 'people pleaser?'

"Do you know what I mean by 'people pleaser'?"

"Oh yes," Abby says. "Absolutely."

"Thought so," Chris says. "There a magic that occurs over-and-over again when I do these events. There's a magnetic attraction that happens between one person in the audience and myself that has me seek him or her out to speak with first thing. So, this morning, it was Abby.

"Abby the lioness, meet Chris the lion," he says with an exaggerated bow towards Abby. "We both be courageous, girl, and . . . we are both people pleasers.

"It's not our fault. Once upon a time, we were innocent victims. And, as grownups now, we can do something about it.

"But it was the hand we were dealt back then. The cards we've been playing with all our lives until now. And it's a pretty poor hand that's kept us from *connecting* authentically with other people in Relationship and Friendship and Partnership, too.

"The only thing we thought we could do to win with a hand like we were delt was to bluff and hope the other players buy our lie and fold.

"So, Abby, grab your seat, and everyone, like I promised you earlier, I'll tell you my story.

"It was a dark and stormy night," Chris begins. "Actually, it was a blue-sky, picture-postcard afternoon. The stormy part would start soon and go on much later.

"I walked to school, and when I'd come home in the afternoon, my mom always met me at the back door with a smile and a hug. The back door led right to the kitchen and she'd always have something for me to eat. That's how I got to be as big as I am," Chris said with a sly smile.

"But this day was different. Door opened. No mom. No smile, no hug, no treat to eat. That had never happened before in my eight-year-old memory, and an alarm bell went off in me immediately.

"So, I moved slowly into the house. Cautiously. Based on the evidence I already had, I was on kid's high alert. Something had to be wrong. And I was right. Something was.

"The house felt eerie. Empty. The air was heavy. Sticky. It was weird.

"There was only one sound. Far away. Weeping.

"I sneaked on tip-toes through the house from the back to the front. Super quietly, but on full alert, because I didn't know what to expect and thought it best if I was both alert and invisible. I was tense from head to toe.

"The crying was coming from my mother's bedroom at the very front of the house, and the closer I got to her door, the louder it got. It was whimpering, not wailing, but plenty loud enough.

"I opened the door as soundlessly as I knew how. Unfortunately, the un-oiled hinges didn't completely cooperate, but I could have used a battering ram, because my mother was curled up in a ball on her bed—as an adult I now know that's the 'fetal position'—with her face buried in the pillow sobbing. She didn't move when I first came in.

"I knew my mother needed me, so I was there to comfort her, like she always comforted me when I was hurt and crying. But I wasn't even through the door when her sobbing became hysterical crying, and she lifted her head out of the pillow and literally screamed at me, 'Leave me alone! Just leave me alone!'

"Her words hit me like a gut punch. *BAM!* Sound familiar Abby?

"I'd been rejected before: Classmates, teammates, teachers, peers, but *never, ever* by my mom. Knocked the air right out of me. *POW!* The little knight in shining armor just got knocked clean off his white horse, and the lady in distress he was riding to save did the knocking. *BOOM!*

"I backed up. One stutter step. Then another. Then I turned and fled.

"What the hell did I do wrong?

"Okay, I didn't think that. We were a card-carrying, church-going family. I would never say 'hell.' Nobody ever cursed in our family. But I was sure confused. My stomach was churning. Knotted one moment. Unraveling the next. Knotted again.

"I ran to my room, and following my mother's example perfectly, I curled up in a ball on the bed, buried my face in my pillow and started crying my eyes out.

"I was in shock. My mother had never, ever screamed at me like that before. I had no idea what I did wrong, but I sure knew I'd messed up big time.

"I was shaking like a leaf. All I knew to do was to pray, 'Please God, make my daddy come home now. Right away. Right now God.' I knew my daddy would make everything all right. He always did. He was our rock. 'Come home, Daddy. Please come home. Now!'

"He did, but instead of making things all right, they got worse. Fast. Lots worse.

"Dad burst in the house, and he was frantic. 'Let me explain,' he kept yelling over and over.

"My mother shot out of the bedroom, throwing my dad's clothes at him, screaming at him to 'Get out! Leave. Get out! You've ruined our family.'

"As I said, we were a good Christian family, and we never used swear words, but my mom and dad pulled 'em all out that night. They called each other every foul name in the book, and I'll bet some nobody'd ever heard before. I sure hadn't.

"Since my dad and I had both been rejected and attacked by this crazy woman who had taken over my mother's body, I wanted to take his side, but even though I didn't know what the words 'discretion' and 'valor' meant, I knew enough that avoiding a dangerous situation was the most sensible thing to do, so I escaped to my room.

"The battle raged outside for hours. I'm not making that up. They yelled and screamed, and my mom threw things at him, ripped up my dad's mom's picture, and broke anything she could that he loved and valued. And she threw his clothes out the door. Two hours. Maybe more. Then, suddenly, it all stopped. Deathly silence. Emphasis on *deathly*.

"I didn't stay hidden in my room, because I was such a wise child. I was huddled in the corner hugging my pillow and didn't move, because I was such a scared little kid. I'd never been so afraid. Haven't been that way again to this day.

"Eventually, my dad came into my room and told me everything was going to be all right. Like I said, he was our rock. He told me that he and my mother wanted me to come out on the porch. It was a big house with a porch that wrapped all the way around. Come out and we'd talk and they'd make it all okay.

"I didn't really believe him. I was right not to.

"Mom sat to one side. Dad on the other. Me in the middle. The monkey in the middle.

"It was tense, but calm, for a brief second—before my mother exploded shrieking at my father, 'Tell him! Tell him! Tell him what you've done to our family!'

"It was all downhill from there, and by downhill, I mean a sheer 90-degree drop straight down to hell.

"My mother accused my father of cheating on her. I didn't know what that meant. I did learn that my aunt called my mother and told her my father was meeting with some other woman. My mom went on a stakeout like they did on cop shows to see for herself. She saw.

"Mom accused. Dad defended.

"Twenty-seven years of marriage down the drain. She didn't understand.

"How could he? She didn't have all the facts.

"Look what he's done to our family. She's mistaken.

"Push-pull. Pull-push. But all of that was just leading up to the grand finale. Can you guess what that was?

"They laid it all on me.

"Tell him to leave, Chris. Tell him!" Mom insisted.

"Tell her you want daddy to stay. Tell her!" my dad pleaded.

"They were kidding. Right? An eight-year-old little boy—a scared kid who'd spent the last six hours crying, confused, turned up-side down, inside-out, and freaking-out—whose entire life was all wrapped up in loving and being loved by the very mother and father who were sitting there demanding he make *that* decision. Right there. Right then. Is that your final answer?

"I wanted to choose dad. No, I wanted it to be mom. No, I wanted dad. No I . . .

"Bitter that *I* was the one that had to choose. Resentful. Wanting to pick them both. Not knowing what else to do, I flipped a coin in my mind and it came up mom.

"So, through my tears and sobs, I told my dad to leave.

"I will never, ever forget the look on his face.

"I instantly regretted saying it and asked him to forgive me. He wouldn't. He never did as long as he lived. I reached out to hug him, but he pushed me away.

"My mother was triumphant, gloating—and I resented her for that.

"So, I spent the rest of my life as long as they lived—they're both gone now—always and only ever telling each of them what I thought they wanted to hear.

"My strategy was simple: If the truth had even a long-shot (you know 50 to 1) chance of getting my butt in trouble, of re-experiencing the pain of that night, I'd lie like a rug to avoid it.

"Will my lying make everybody happy? If my answer was 'Yes,' then I'd go for it. If it was 'No,' I'd better come up with something else quick.

"Until I got myself straightened out—and I'll share more about how that happened with you—I had perfected *people pleasing*. I started with my mom and dad and graduated to everybody else in my life. I was an absolute master of both the art and science of the people pleasing game. I was so good I became a pastor—the most people pleasing profession of all.

"Hey . . . people pleasing is a perfect way to *connect* with people. *Is everybody happy!?! Hallelujah!*

"Like an alcoholic with his drinking, it worked great for me—until it didn't work anymore.

"And the reason it didn't and doesn't work is that people pleasing, or any other strategy born of a lie, is manipulation—a clever attempt to control or influence another person or a situation unfairly, or unscrupulously."

Lesson #12

"Any Relationship Based On Manipulation Is Doomed To Fail."

"Have you—any of you—ever observed a Relationship, Friendship, Partnership, or anyone who achieved a position of Leadership that was based on manipulation?

"How'd that go for them? How'd that work out? How did you *feel* about that, and how did you feel about *them?*"

Chris pauses, searching the audience. "I see some of you know from whence I speak.

"So, Abby, dear lioness, how close was I when I said you and I were people pleasers?"

"Real close," Abby yells out strongly.

"*Roar!* You're becoming more of a lioness all the time," Chris quipped. "And do I know how well that's worked out for you so far?" Chris asks her.

"You do," she shouts back.

To everyone's surprise, including Chris's, Abby stands up and asks for a microphone. Quickly, a team member puts one in her hand.

"Hey everybody," Abby says. "Way out of my comfort zone here—getting my money's worth," she laughs. "Let's turn the tables and acknowledge Chris for his courage to tell us his story. Give him a big hand." And that's exactly what they did. A huge big hand.

Chris spreads his arms wide accepting the truly thunderous applause. He turns day-glow red, and is shaking his head, a tad tearful and laughing at the same time.

When the ovation dies down, Chris says with a big sigh and smile, "Still being a people pleaser, huh, Abby? Only this time, it's authentic. You *are* an inspiration lady. Thank you."

"Wow! That was a first. Wow!"

Lesson #13

True Life Begins Where Your Comfort Zone Ends.

Chris, still laughing and shaking his head, says, "Abby just did something I want us to focus on. It's a cool lesson.

"Remember when she said she was about to do something that was 'out of her comfort zone'?

"So . . . What's a comfort zone?" he asks.

Chris pauses a bit and then says, "I know there's no such thing as a stupid question, but that one comes close, doesn't it?

"It's a place where you're comfortable, obviously. So, something outside of your comfort zone would be anything that's *not* comfortable for you—yes?"

The audience agrees.

"So, let's take a quick look at some of the ways you experience that you're not comfortable: Is there anything that's common to each of your examples of discomfort?"

Chris waits for a response. There is none. After a short pause, Chris continues, "All right. Let me try a different approach. Anybody have a rubber band?"

A woman calls out that she had a hair band. Chris thanks her, but he says he really wanted a rubber band. A few rows back, a guy stood up and said he had one, and came down the aisle and handed it to Chris.

"Thanks," Chris says, "What's your name?"

"Chris," the man says.

"That's a *wonderful* name," Chris says with a laugh, and then asks the audience to give the other Chris a hand.

"Chris," Chris asks, "How do you happen to have a rubber band handy?"

"I wear it on my wrist," Chris tells him.

"Because . . . ?" Chris asks.

"Every time I catch myself having a negative thought, I pull it back and snap it, hard, so it hurts. Trying to train myself to be positive."

"Wow!" Chris exclaims. "What a cool idea. How's that working for ya'?"

"Well, my wrist hurts a lot," and both Chrises break up laughing.

"Now, that deserves another round of applause," Chris says, and the audience clearly agrees.

As the other Chris heads back to his seat, the bigger Chris tells him he'll return the rubber band shortly. Then he holds it high in the air for all to see.

"This," he says, "is a rubber band in its comfort zone."

He turns from side to side, showing the room the rubber band hanging limp from his fingers.

"So, what good is it when it's like this?"

"Not much. Pretty useless, isn't it, just hanging there? But get it out of its comfort zone," and he demonstrates by stretching the rubber band with both hands, "and it's doing what a rubber band was designed to do.

"Now it will hold a bunch of envelopes together or keep a plastic bag in the freezer tight—or . . . whack Chris a good one on the wrist.

"You and I are just like this rubber band. If we stay in our comfort zone, we're not doing what we are designed to do. Ain't much energy in the comfort zone," he says wiggling the limp rubber band in his hand.

Chris takes the rubber band in his two hands and stretches it apart. "This hand," he raises his left hand up, "is my comfort zone. In this hand," he raises his right hand higher, "is the thing I want to do: the desire, dream, might even be something I think I deserve. That's the risk that's in front of me.

"Think of Abby sitting in her comfort zone . . . " Again he raises his left hand holding the rubber band. "Now, this is Abby having the thought to stand up and ask you all to applaud for me." He wiggles his fingers to emphasize his right hand, stretching the rubber band.

"Tension, right? Now . . . " And he stretches both sides of the rubber band way far apart. "This is Abby standing up. Tension big time.

"Abby, let me ask you, did you experience any tension when you thought about standing up?"

"Yes."

"And when you did stand up and started to speak, was there even more tension?"

"Oh yeah!"

"Can you remember how long that lasted Abby?"

"Oh . . . about five seconds or so."

"Really. Your body was created to protect itself by doing everything in its power for you not to endure pain, tension, or stress. However, when you try to get out of your comfort zone—and this is a proven fact—you have only about five seconds to move before your brain-mind begins to talk you out of taking that action. It's just trying to keep you safe. This is why you must act immediately the moment you choose to break out of your comfort zone.

"So, did you experience the energy flowing either time?"

"Yes. Lots. More when I stood up and started to speak."
"Did that energy have you feel *alive?*"
"Yes, it did!" Abby says with conviction. "Not very comfortable, but alive, that's for sure."
"Folks," Chris says, "Life *requires* tension. It's the energy. That's why we speak about being stretched when we grow. Just like this rubber band. Just like Abby.
"*Connection* requires tension. Comfort doesn't. In fact, most all of the time, comfort is the *absence* of tension. No energy. Flat lined.
"There's no growth in your comfort zone. There's no aliveness in your comfort zone. Life begins where your comfort zone ends.
"And I promise you, you ain't makin' no *connections* with anything truly worthwhile from your comfort zone.
"Okay," Chris says, "look . . . "

Lesson #14

"Life Either Happens TO you You or FOR You."

"Bad news about today for you all is now you get to choose. TO or FOR. It's on you from now on. That victim you've been, you can continue to be. It may be years after what initially happened TO you that it comes around on the guitar in a way that you can choose to use it FOR you.

"Took me a long, long time to turn that night from *hell* with my mom and dad that happened TO me into a *heavenly* happening FOR me.

"But you can choose—always and in all ways—to live your life FOR the highest good of yourself and all concerned. No matter what happens TO you.

"And I highly recommend it.

"Time for a break? Let's do it. A quickie. Eleven minutes too quick? Good. Let's go."

Then music begins to play.

Everybody is in their seats. On time. The music stops. The theater is silent.

Seconds ticked by. Still there is silence. People begin to shift uncomfortably in their seats. Whispers of, "What's he up to? What's happening?' murmured around the theater.

Then, Chris's voice speaks, more like echoes, but he is nowhere to be seen. "Thou shalt have no other gods before me."

After a few seconds Chris comes down the aisle from the very back of the theater.

"Scared ya' didn't I?" he says with a laugh.

"Bet ya' thought you were back in church or the synagogue. No worries, mates," Chris quips with his best Australian accent, which is bad enough to be comical.

He keeps speaking as he walks to the front of the room. "I'm an ex-pastor. Emphasis on *ex*. But I'm still a preacher, teacher, sometimes even a screecher. But please, not to worry. No sermon, just references.

"What do you think is THE #1 cause of our *DISconnectedness*? What gets in the way of you and me *connecting* with all the nouns in our lives—all those persons, places and things?"

Chris is at the front now. He lets his question hang in the air for a bit. The audience yells out a number of answers. The moment he hears someone say the word, Chris jumps on it.

"Ego," he says. "Which is what I meant when I said, 'Thou shalt have no other gods before me.'

"For too many people today, their ego is their God."

"Ego. A very little word for a HUGE idea. And just like my opinion not being true and not being false, we in the personal growth biz often labeled anything 'ego' as bad. Not so. Ego isn't good or bad—as Shakespeare would tell us—'but thinking makes it so.'

"Having a healthy sense of self-esteem—which is part of your ego—is a good thing. Hey, I said you were special, one in a gazillion. There's an ego boost for ya."

"All kinds of things fall under the broad heading of ego," Chris explains. "It's like sex. Procreation—making sure human life on Earth continues, having babies, the intimacy and ecstasy of making love—that's all sex. But so are abuse and pornography.

"It's what we do with our egos that has them serve for the highest good of ourselves and everybody involved—or not.

"It's how we handle, manage, relate to, or use our egos that enables us to *connect* or be *DISconnected*.

"One way I've seen people kill *connection* in Relationships, Friendships, Partnerships and their own Leadership, is their ego's need to be right."

"Want a short cut to *connecting* powerfully and positively with everybody and everything in your life . . . "

"Give up your right to be right."

"Really. Who cares? What difference does it make? And making other people wrong makes a big bad difference!"

"I'll say that another way . . . "

"Quit playing God."

"Know why people say 'God Knows'?" Chris asks. "Because He's the only one who does. We don't. But how many conversations have you been in lately where it was all about one person wins and the other is the looser?"

"Agree. Disagree. I'm right. She's wrong. My dog's better than your dog. That's competition, NOT conversation.

"And it sure as heaven cannot create any *connection* for the *highest good.*

"The *lowest bad* is more like it.

"Huge *DISconnect.* Yuge!"

"And while I'm ranting away here, I'm going to say one more thing about playing God. Sometimes we the people do it with the absolute best intentions in the world. We do this in church all the time.

"Pray for a cure for so-and-so's mother who has cancer . . . For the family that just lost their home to foreclosure, God please bring them a new one. Pray for the refugees, feeding the hungry, saving the victims of this or that disaster.

"Nobody on this planet would dare fault you for that—except me . . . "

He lets his remark hang in the air.

"I do not know what's best for ANYbody. As I said, God knows, and He—or whatever higher power you believe is the Source of all Creation—is the only one who does.

"When I pray for people—what the church calls 'intercession'—I always end my prayer with the same thing. I ask God to bless this person . . .

"For the highest good of themselves and all concerned."

"That way, I'm honoring God and whatever HE has planned, what He thinks best. Not what I think best. I call that my insurance policy. Now I'm covered.

"Have you ever—or know of someone who has—experienced adversity? Gone through it, learned the tough lessons, been made stronger and wiser, refined their character, become a more and better human being, because of their trials and tribulations?

"Of course, we have specific desires, dreams, and hopes for people—and for ourselves. Perfect. Have them. Speak them. Pray them. But always add, 'For the highest good of that person and all concerned,' even and especially when that person I'm praying for is myself."

Chris pauses a moment and then walks up on stage. Behind him, the big screen comes to life with the simple text graphic...

Foundational Principles for Being a Master Connector.

H.E.L.P. and L.O.V.E.

"Professor Dorrity's Connection 101. Class is now in session," he announced. "First, a request—and some of you will find this really strange, because it goes against a lifetime of your experience. But, you know by now I love doing that, so . . .

"Please, DO NOT TAKE NOTES.

"How's *that* grab ya'?" Chris asks with a big smile.

"You've been taking notes all through middle school, high school, college, and grad school—if you did that and those. You've taken notes in every seminar and workshop you've ever attended. Am I right?

"So, how'd that work for you? How useful and valuable was all that diligent note-taking?

"I'll bet some of you even kept all those notes. Ever look at them? Do you remember them?

"Let me tell you a story. A friend of mine's wife grew up in the former Soviet Union, like Katya did. And also like Katya—I'm guessing here—she went to the music conservatory. Did you do that, too, Katya?"

Chris looks around the audience to learn where Katya is sitting. She is in the front row and answers him with a loud, "Yes!"

"In her last year at conservatory," he continues, "my friend's wife had a particularly demanding professor of music theory. Her exams were absolute torture. Her students had to recall tons of specific details: Who said what, when, how did that apply to this piece, that one, which composer did what . . . Like that. *Whew!*

"So, in that class everybody took reams of super-copious notes.

"One day, my friend's wife gets to class, and she had forgot her notebook. No pen either. She asked around, begged around actually, to borrow pen and paper, but not one of the other students had any to spare. So . . . she was, as we say in the West, *screwed*.

"She had no choice, but to sit there and listen without the aid of taking notes.

"When exam time came, sure enough the biggest section of the test was on *that* class that she had no notes to study from. When she saw that on the test, her heart sank. She just knew she was going to fail.

"Her first surprise was that that part of the exam was actually the easiest one for her to complete. Second surprise: *She aced it!* Best grade she'd ever received in that class.

"Here's the deal," Chris says.

"We learned in school that two objects cannot occupy the same place in space at the same time. Okay, the quantum physics kids have tried to debunk that with their theoretical mathematics, but for all practical purposes, that's the way it is in our world of people, places and things. I can't park my car in the same space at the same time as you park yours.

"And I say you cannot listen—REALLY LISTEN—when you're taking notes. You can do one, or the other, not both at the same time.

"Look and see if this makes sense: When you listen, really listen with your full and complete attention, you'll have total recall. You can remember what you heard, because you were *fully and completely listening.*

"Remember what my friend's wife remembered in music class. I say she accomplished all that remarkable recalling on the exam because she had no choice but to listen. Not take notes. Fully and completely listen.

"Now, to ease you mind about this, we're giving you handouts right now of all the slides you see up here. And if there's a gem I come up with, and you want to jot that down, please, feel free. But spend the most of your time LISTENING, really listening. Okay?

"Great. Lesson One." And this image appears on the screen behind Chris.

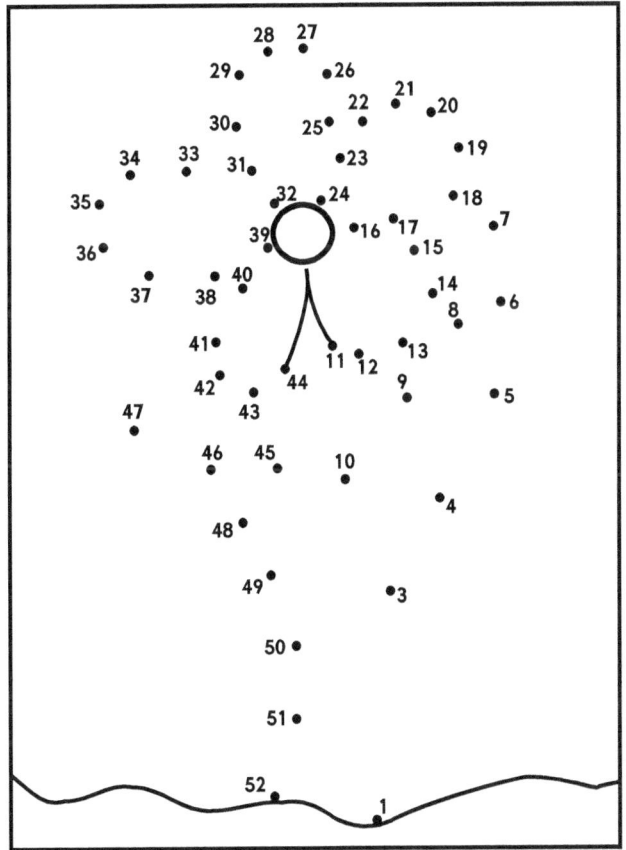

"Remember playing '*Connect* the Dots' as a little kid?" Chris asks, pointing at the image up on the screen.

"You'd take your crayon, start at number one, then draw a line connecting to number two and then three, then 10 and 21 and . . . Bingo. A daisy. Or a teddy bear. Or . . . Geeze. Look at that. They forgot number 2.

"Just like in the real world. Sometimes you just have to imagine where the next dot to *connect* to is supposed to be." He laughs.

"So, Lesson One to becoming a Master *Connector* is go back to what it was like as a little kid and *connect* the dots. Simple, isn't it?

"All right. Now. First Secret . . . " And the slide appeared on the screen. ". . . is . . . "

H. E. L. P.

"The H. stands for . . . "

HONESTY

"And honesty *is* . . . ?" Chris says, letting the question hang in the air.

Many in the audience fill in the blank, calling out, " . . . the best policy."

"Indeed," Chris says. "Thanks to all you Ben Franklin fans for filling in the blank.

"Remember back when we spoke about 'people pleasing,' and I said the basic reason that doesn't work is that it's a lie. It's dishonest and dishonesty leads directly to *DISconnection.* Or, creating the kind of manipulation *connection* that's doomed to fail. It's 'Honor among thieves.' Nice work if you can get it—and you *can* get it if you try, but is that the kind of home or work life *you* want?

"Putting honesty first is the way to make *connections* that last."

"The deepest regrets I have in my life," Chris admits, "all have one thing in common—I was dishonest.

"'Oh, what a tangled web we weave when first we practice to deceive,' Sir Walter Scott said.

"Let's get down an' dirty about honesty. Bottom-line.

"Honesty is just easier than lying. Have you ever lied and then struggled to remember exactly what you said in order to maintain the lie? Man, that's hard work.

"And you *will* get caught. You know that.

"Look, a bad truth is better than the best lie. People are 100 times more upset when they find out you lied to them than they are when you tell them the truth, even when it hurts.

"Instead of telling your kids that grandpa died, you say, 'He went to sleep,' and then you wonder why they're so scared to go to bed at night.

"And worst of all . . . The #1 reason to be honest, always and in all ways . . . is TRUST.

"Okay, watch your *instant* reaction to what I say next.

"I hand you my business card, and it reads, 'Chris Dorrity. LIAR.'

"Whoa! *Right?*

"Any difference for you if my card read, 'Chris Dorrity. TRUTH TELLER'?"

He pauses a bit before going on.

"Is there anyone in your life, any person or business or institution that once you did, but now you don't, trust? What will he, she, or it have to do to regain your trust? Is it even possible?

"Honesty is the keystone of *connection*."

"A *DIS*honest *connection is a DIS*connection.

"'This above all,' Bill Shakespeare told us, 'to thine own self be true.' Being who and how you are—who and how you REALLY are—it's not just the best policy. It's the ONLY policy.

"Have you ever pretended to be something or someone other than you really are so that someone will like you, or to get a job, maybe even have fall in love with you? How'd that work for ya'?

"Let's be honest here. I'll lead the way. I've lied in school. I've lied to get a job. I've lied to get a girl. So how'd all of those work out for ya' Chris?" He pauses. "I won't make you guess the answer. They didn't. Not a one.

"When I began this CONNECT . . . OR DIE project, a very successful pastor told me, 'Chris, you've got to clean up your act big time. Get a slick suit and tie. Lose that good-old-boy accent. Get rid of the 'dems' and 'dose' and speak the King's English.

"Wow, extreme Chris Dorrity makeover. Can you imagine what went through my mind? How I felt when he told me that?

"It's a blessing for me that on my very next phone call I told my friend, who was also a coach, what the pastor said and he immediately told me, *'Don't you dare!'*

"He said, 'Chris, you *are* a good old boy. A card-carrying Georgia preacher, cracker, peach. Your shirttail's out, and your hats on backwards. You're WWE and NASCAR. Ribs, cheese grits, catfish and red beans. That's who and how you are buddy. That's Chris Dorrity.

"You wear your heart on your sleeve, but not because it covers up your tattoo. You're a character. One-of-a-kind. What you see is what you get—authentic Southern-fried. The real deal. Don't you dare hide that!

"'I can promise you,' he told me, 'some folks won't like that or you. Not at all. But they're not *your* people. Those that do like you will *love* you. They'll love it that you're authentic and real, because that'll give them permission to be authentic and real, too. That's just another of the gifts you give people Chris.'

"So . . . " Chris said, with his arms spread wide apart palms up, "what you see is what you get. This is me. And this me wants to *connect* with the real, authentic you."

Chris moves to the front edge of the stage and asks, "What's one thing about this *honest conversation* you appreciate most?

And tell me what makes you say that—what's most important about that for you?

"Just to remind," he adds. "That first question is for your left brain, your rational/logical conscious mind. The second one is for your right brain to answer. Your subconscious. Your intuition and imagination. It's for your heart."

Chris engages with a number of people. Each stands up, says their names, gets spirited applause, and has a thoughtful conversation-*connection* about honesty with Chris.

"Now," he says, "don't answer me on this one. Just give it some thought. What do you suppose I'm demonstrating when I engage with you all like this—asking what you appreciate and why?"

Chris pauses a moment, then walks back a bit and off to the side of the big screen, and the next slide appears.

ENERGY

"You know all about this one—yes?" Chris asks. "Been there, done that with the exercise we did with what's the worst thing that happened and the best thing that happened.

"Positive Energy. From this day forward make it part of your job description. The world is full of Energy Vampires that suck the life out of us, so we must bring the positive energy with us everywhere we go.

"Positive Energy is an ATTITUDE of finding the good, what's right, in every person and situation.

"Positive Energy is APPRECIATION for life and the things in this life that *connect* us all.

"Bringing Positive Energy to every *connection* party you go to makes people feel great about themselves—and when that happens, how do you think they feel about you?

"Positive Energy is ACCEPTED. You deliver the energy, and someone else will always pick it up.

"True, you can *connect* negatively. Birds of a feather flock together for a reason. People who love to complain seem to have a great time hanging with other whiners and moaners.

"So, it's pretty simple: What's the *quality* of *connection* you want in your life? In your Relationships and Friendships?

"And what's the legacy of all the leaders throughout history who've brought bad, negative energy into the world?

"Remember, what you focus on becomes the center of your life. So, if you want an energy-draining, negative and complaining life . . . seek and ye shall find. If you don't, then knock on this door . . . " And the next slide appears.

Validate Don't Violate

"Make that a rule you commit to upholding in all your conversations and *connections* with people.

"Seek value, instead of finding fault.

"Focus on what's right, instead of what's wrong.

"Concentrate on the solution, not the problem.

"As soon as you can, take the attention off the pain, and celebrate the pleasure.

"Accept people as you find them, and they will remain as you found them. Recognize and appreciate the greatness you see and sense in them, and they will become as great as they are capable of becoming.

"Or as the old song my grandma used to sing . . . " And Chris actually sings the words.

Accentuate the positive
Eliminate the negative
Latch on to the affirmative
Don't mess with
Mister In-Between

"Mr., Mrs., Miss., and Mz. In-Between are not Master *Connectors!* So don't mess with them," he laughed and moved to the very front edge of the stage to address the audience to ask them his next two "pet" questions.

The slide appears.

LAUGHTER

"Can we please have some FUN with each other?" Chris literally begs the audience, clasping his hands together in a pleading manner.

"Scientific fact; laughter *connects* us. Not sure who said this, but I wholeheartedly agree, 'Laughter is the closest distance between two people.'

"Laughter *Connects* Us. Instantly!"

"Hey, did you hear the one about . . . ? Tell a joke, say something funny, tell one on yourself, and people feel good about you. Right away. Back to that 'know-like-and-trust' thing. Humor makes that happen.

"And like listening, humor and the smiles and laughter that it generates not only *connects,* it also *heals!* Laughter is indeed the best medicine.

"Just more scientific fact: Researchers have proven humor reduces pain by releasing those feel-good, pain-killing hormones called endorphins. Humor strengthens our immune system by increasing production of T-cells, interferon and protective proteins called globulins. And laughter decreases stress by lowering cortisol levels, returning the body to a more calm and relaxed state.

"So . . . aren't you impressed by Dr. Christopher Dorrity's expert scientific-medical knowledge?" Chris asks.

"*That* was humor." He says with a laugh. "So, are we more *connected* now?" The audience was giggling, too.

"By the way, former *Pastor* Dorrity knows that way back in the Old Testament they knew all about the healing power of humor. Proverbs 17:22. 'A merry heart doeth good like a medicine.'

"Now, there's a dot-dot-dot after HUMOR. I misuse ellipses a bunch, but they're there to let you know something's left out, and it's coming. Now.

"A close-cousin of HUMOR," Chris says, "is the COMPLIMENT.

"A compliment shows you noticed. You care. You're interested in *them*."

"A compliment makes people feel good about themselves. Makes people feel better than before they met up with you.

"You can't compliment someone unless you're paying attention to that person. And it's a truth that people don't care how much you know until they know how much you care.

"When you compliment someone you are instantly labeled by them as generous person. And that's a very good thing.

"A true and meaningful compliment is an expression of admiration, approval, gratitude, trust, appreciation, and hope. And I emphasize that '*true and meaningful*' bit. Flattery is 'fake news' and doesn't cut it. Only sincerity rings true. And sincerity is impossible to fake.

"You look great! Have you been working out? Where'd you get that dress? Jacket? Those cool shoes? Who cuts your hair?

"And notice those were questions. Curiosity is the best compliment of all. Asking creates instant *connection*. Try it. You'll like it. And . . . the other person will like you, too."

After he speaks with a number of people in the audience about humor and compliments, Chris calls out, "Next!" And a new slide appears.

PRESENCE

"To *connect* truly and authentically with other people, you must be fully present, focused on that person, and hold yourself accountable for being so. And in this day and age of sleeping with your iPhone, that's tough to do.

"High-Tech doesn't have to be the enemy of High-Touch, but it often is." As Chris says that, this image flashes on the screen behind him.

"Funny." he says pointing up at the picture of the family all on their phones. "But not really. Actually pretty sad.

"Being on the phone, or checking your email, or . . .

"Have you ever been to a sports bar—you know that restaurant where there are 20 TVs screens all around the place, and no matter where you sit you can't help but notice three or four of them? Talk about distraction. Those things are attention magnets—right? You can't help but be completely *DISconnected* from people even sitting right next to them in a place like that.

"But the most widespread *place like that* for distraction and *DISconnection,* is the space between our ears. Don't know about you, but I've got a few hundred TV screens in my head.

"If you and I are speaking, and I have any thoughts other than hearing the words you're saying, I am NOT there. NOT all present and accounted for. That's NOT Be Here Now. That's Gone Somewhere Whenever.

"In order to be absolutely present at all times with someone," Chris explains, "you must build rapport with them."

Rapport is POWER.

"I promise you, there's somebody out there in this world who has exactly what you need—*connections,* capital, knowledge, and so forth—to accomplish all of your dreams. And the way to have them be happy and willing to help you is first to build rapport with them.

"Rapport means total responsiveness and you cannot be totally RESPONSIVE TO OTHERS UNLESS YOU ARE FULLY PRESENT.

"Rapport is created between two people who feel as if they are a lot like each other. Rapport is lost when people feel like they are not alike at all. Rapport does not always work alone, but when you Listen, Watch, and Learn, you build deeper *connections,* and your Rapport becomes *powerful!*

"And there is one—and only one—key that unlocks all the secret doors of having those powerful deeper *connections,* and that's . . . "

As Chris speaks, the next slide appears on the big screen.

L. O. V. E.

"The first letter in LOVE stands for . . . LISTEN.

"My friend John Fogg wrote the book on Listening. He says the number one problem in the world today is . . .

Nobody's Listening.

"And John admits he doesn't always Listen, even though he's been teaching it to people for more than 25 years! What that should tell you is Listening is a life-long learning experience. We can all and always become better Listeners.

"In John's book, he points out that beyond being a scientifically proven fact that people aren't Listening to each other, you can simply test this out for yourself, in your own life. In the book, he asks—and I want you right now to ask yourselves . . .

"Are the nations of the world Listening to each other?

"Do our elected local or national leaders really Listen to us?

"Does your employer? Your customers . . . clients . . . co-workers . . . ? The cop on the corner? The guy behind the counter? Are *they* Listening?

"Are any of you married—in a committed relationship? Does your partner *really* Listen to you?

"Then John asks these two killer questions, which as a parent I just love. 'Anybody have kids? What's your biggest complaint about them? And what do they always say about you?'

"You don't LISTEN to me!"

"Folks," Chris says, "Most people do not Listen and I agree with John, it is THE biggest source of *DISconnect* on the planet.

"NOT Listening is the #1 reason most people struggle and suffer in Relationships, Friendships, Partnerships, and with our own and other's Leadership.

"We cannot know, like, and trust each other unless we truly Listen to each other.

"It's why so often we feel empty. Abandoned and . . . ALONE.

"Abby, Dear, are you *Listening?*" Chris asks with a big smile.

"And look," Chris says, "Listening really Listening—is not easy. I can promise you that a half-hour of fully and completely Listening to someone will leave you as tired as if you had run a few miles.

"But if you want to be a Master *Connector,* Listening will be your number one most useful, valuable and powerful skill.

"Oh . . . and did I say that *Listening* heals?"

"It does. We live in a world that's dying—literally—to be heard."

And the next slide appears on the screen

OBSERVE

"And . . . Chris continues as the slide comes up, "we live in a world that's dying—literally—to be *seen*.

"CONNECT . . . OR DIE.

"You can save lives with your Listening and Observing." Rapport is created by a feeling of commonality and with it comes a spark. Words don't always work but . . . Listening and Watching always *connects*.

"Robbins Research teaches us that there are four keys to proper Listening and Observing.

"Number one is **Eye Contact.** By maintaining good eye contact, you're demonstrating to your partner that you are fully engaged and interested in what he or she is saying. A good guideline to follow is the 80/20 rule, in which 80 percent of the time your eyes are meeting your speaking partner's eyes, and 20 percent of the time, your eyes are roaming as you're thinking and gathering information.

"It's up to you to stop your mind from shifting away from the conversation and to be truly present. Not only will you be able to more fully absorb what your partner says, but also you'll be able to respond in kind, which makes them feel appreciated and understood.

"This next one is so important," Chris says. "Nonverbal Feedback.

"There's nothing worse than speaking to someone who gives no visual feedback. It's like talking to a wall.

"Make the effort to give the occasional nod, smile, or some other sign of recognition to your partner. These nonverbal cues may seem trivial, but they have tremendous impact by showing your interest, understanding and involvement in the conversation—and more importantly, in them.

"And last, but not . . . " Chris adds with a pause . . . "Position.

"When you're speaking one-on-one with someone, position your body in a way that creates a safe and welcoming space for him or her to speak openly with you.

"Lean slightly in, open up your chest, pull your shoulders back, and fold your hands gently in your lap or on the table in front of you. If you are standing, form a reversed hand steeple in which the fingers come together to form a point. When someone steeples in the lap area, it means they are confident about what they are hearing.

"It was 50 years ago that Dr. Milton Erickson. Erickson, a medical psychologist and a hypnotherapist, became intrigued by the human conscious and sub-conscious mind.

"Dr. Erickson had polio and was confined to a wheelchair. He spent most of his days studying people and how they interacted with their surroundings. Through his observations, he learned that the sub-conscious mind was way more powerful.

"The sub-conscious is that thing that makes our heart beat 100,000 times a day. Dr. Erickson recognized rapport as being powerful when he noticed people mirroring others by Listening and Observing.

"Think about it. In your mind, name a person you like and a person you don't like. I guarantee you like those who are most like you or how you would like to be. I bet you don't like the ones who are not like you or how you wish not to be.

"Dr. Erickson would accommodate his patients by mirroring their body movement, their tones, and breathing patterns. This gave his patients an immediate and deep sense of *connection* to him which in return gave him the ability to lead them.

"Okay," Chris says, "did all that sound like a lecture? It did to me." He laughs and says in a loud voice as he points to the screen, "Next slide class!"

VULNERABILITY

"So, Abby, George, Katya, and all the rest of you remarkable people who stood or sat and spoke with me today . . . Thank you for your honesty, candor, bravery and most of all . . . your *willingness* to BE VULNERABLE.

"You heard me use the phrase 'willing and able' a number of times today. Every one of us is *able* to be vulnerable. The question is . . . always is . . . are you willing?

"Willing means ready, eager, or prepared to do something.

"Take a look at your life. How ready, eager, and prepared are you to be *vulnerable?*"

"IF you notice that you're not always *willing* to be vulnerable, I highly recommend a visit to Dr. Vulnerabilty herself, best-selling author, Brené Brown. Her video, *The Power of Vulnerability*, is one of the top ten most *connected*—by which I mean watched—TED Talks in the world.

"Professor Brown teaches that we commonly, '... associate vulnerability with emotions we want to *avoid*, such as fear, shame, and uncertainty.' When we do that, she says, '... we lose sight of the fact that vulnerability is also the birthplace of joy, belonging, creativity, authenticity, and love.'

"Oh my!" Chris exclaims. "I want a piece of that and those—joy, belonging, creativity, authenticity, and love. I want a BIG piece of all of them!

"I don't know about you..." he says, but stops. "Well, that's not true. I probably *do* know about you, because most people I've known did not grow up learning to be vulnerable. I didn't. Did you?

"Boys don't cry. Suck it up. Tough it out. Never let 'em see you sweat. In the South, fathers frequently beat vulnerability out of their good-old little boys.

"And mothers taught their daughters to build 20 foot-high walls around their hearts to keep out the pain. Of course, Mom meant well. No mother wants her little girl to struggle and suffer like she did—and most moms did.

"Even though our parents were a major influence . . .

"WE are our own best DON'T BE VULNERABLE teachers."

"Today, research has proven what you and I learned in our hard-knocks schools and homes and lives: We will do anything to *avoid pain*—way more than what we'll do to *seek pleasure*.

"And this is another of those 'It's Not Your Fault' deals.

"Our hunter-gatherer ancestors got the message early on that the pleasure of those ripe berries could always wait, but the pain of that angry bear who saw them as lunch was often fatal. So, to survive, humans learned to stay far away from any and every potential source of pain. DNA encoding like that is hard to change.

"One secret to success is learning how to use pain and pleasure, instead of having pain and pleasure use you.

"Being vulnerable is a risk. A big risk. It takes courage. Big Courage. Like Abby showed us.

"And I have to be vulnerable with you here. I am NOT good at it. Actually, I suck.

"Why? Fear.

"Most people see being vulnerable as WEAKNESS. To be open and exposed is to be weak, but . . .

"Being Vulnerable Is Our Greatest *Source* of Courage."

"That's a scientific fact."

"When the researchers asked for examples of vulnerability, they got: the first date after a divorce . . . starting my own company . . . taking responsibility for something that goes wrong . . . sitting with my wife who has stage 3 breast cancer . . . and making plans for our child's future. That's tough stuff," Chris explains.

"Vulnerability is defined as uncertainty, risk, and emotional exposure. It is showing up and being seen without any guarantees. But courage comes from vulnerability. Putting yourself out there knowing sometimes you will fail. Now that, my friends, is COURAGE.

"It's one of those things we are never taught to do; however, if we embraced it, it could lead to our greatest source of power.

"So, what am I afraid of? That you'll think I'm weak. That you'll lose respect for me. You won't admire me. That you'll think the guy on stage doesn't have it all together. That you'll choose not to *connect* with me.

"Man, I do hate to be embarrassed in front of people. In a word, I avoid the pain of *shame* like a live grenade.

"Brené Brown taught me something really powerful about that. She said that guilt was, 'I *made* a mistake.' And shame was, 'I *am* a mistake.'

"So . . . " Chris says, and takes a deep breath.

"What I know to do about that—about training myself to be vulnerable—is to take it in baby steps. Take a small risk before I try a giant one. Tell the truth, like I just did with you now.

"Honestly exposing myself in front of 1,500 people is not all that risky, because you paid to see me. I know I can *connect* with each one of you by being vulnerable. Heart-to-heart and let the chips fall.

"Be the people pleaser who takes the chance that somebody won't be pleased."

"And to hope... And trust... In God... And in y'all... That by my doing that, some of you will be encouraged to risk vulnerability next time you get the chance."

This time, the audience didn't need anyone to encourage them. Before Chris has barely finished speaking, they are on their feet with spontaneous applause.

When the clapping, hollering, and hooting have died down and people take their seats, Chris says, "And the E in L.O.V.E. stands for..."

EMPATHY

"So . . . What is empathy and how does it work with *connecting* to others?

"It's often defined as the ability to recognize other people's emotions—and it's linked with the ability to imagine what someone else might be thinking or feeling.

"Researchers say there are two types of empathy: Affective and Cognitive.

"Affective empathy refers to the awareness we get in response to others' emotions. For instance, we see this when we're mirroring what another person is feeling. We also experience this when we pick-up on another person's fear or anxiety.

"Cognitive empathy is seeing situations from another person's perspective. It refers to the ability to relate and comprehend other people's emotions.

"Why Practice Empathy?"

"Because empathy is a key foundation of our human existence. It's what allows us to follow the Golden Rule. And it helps first if we can put ourselves in the shoes of those in whom we come in contact with.

"Empathy is what happens naturally when we *connect* heart-to-heart.

"Empathy is also the basis for successful Relationships, because it helps us understand the perspective, the point of view, needs, wants and intentions of others. Empathy allows us to see where people are coming from, so that we can respond appropriately to the situation.

"Empathy feels WITH the other person, rather than feeling sorry for them."

"Being empathetic means we invest into another person's world and *connect* with them on a feeling awareness level.

"You don't always have to agree with the person or understand completely where he or she is coming from to be able to empathize with them. You just need to be present, and support what they're experiencing.

"So, just to recap . . . " and as Chris is speaking the familiar rhythmic beat of reggae music dances softly from the speakers. " In order to become a Master *Connector* and create meaningful, lasting, and successful Relationships, Friendships, Partnerships and bring out our own Leadership we must H.E.L.P. and L.O.V.E . . .

"We're going to take a 31-minute working break," Chris announces. "Here's what I want you to do . . .

"After you dance up the aisle and outside into the lobby, pick a partner, somebody you didn't know before you came here today, and a person you haven't met or spoken with yet.

"Say 'Hi.' Introduce yourself. You can give them a round of applause or a heart-to-heart hug if you want. Then, pick one of you to go first.

"What I want you to do is to choose someone in your life—you may know the person personally or not. It could be a character from history, or an author you appreciate, someone from politics or entertainment or sports—one person who you know is a Master *Connector*.

"Then, I want you to tell your partner three things you admire most about that Master *Connector*, and briefly—really, *briefly*—explain what makes that one specific quality you admire about them so admirable, so worthy of your esteem. Do that for all three things you admire about him or her.

"So, you got all that?" Chris asks. "Any questions about your work on the break?" There are none, so Chris announces with a sweeping wind-up and fist pump, "It's party time Mon!" And the audience fills the aisles and dances out of the theater.

At the 31-minute mark, the theater is full; folks are in their seats, Chris is down on the floor standing right up front, and he begins.

"Thanks for being on time. You *are* a special group. I appreciate that and you. And *y'all*." He says *y'all* in an exaggerated Southern accent.

"Now, forgive me for playing a bit of a trick on you. You just took part in a game you didn't know you were playing. Mea culpa," Chris says. He spreads his arms wide apart with his palms up, as if asking for forgiveness, which, is actually what he's doing.

"You'll understand why I didn't tell you about it before hand when I explain.

"It's called the 'Mirror Game.' And it's one of my favorite ways to *connect* with people.

"When you ask people to name a person they admire, and to tell you a couple of things they admire most about that person, and why that matters to them—what makes those qualities so important for them—they will be telling you all about . . . *themselves.*"

Chris silently lets that idea sink in.

"You see," he continues after a bit, "you and I can only identify those qualities in another person that we possess in ourselves.

"That's why it's called the 'Mirror Game.' It's a reflection of our true selves."

"Oh sure, we may not have perfected those qualities. We may aspire to have more or better of that quality in our selves. But rest assured, we are talking about us.

"So if you'd picked Abraham Lincoln, and told your partner you admired Abe's honesty . . . Guess what?

"If you talked about Mother Teresa, and spoke about how much you admired her loving kindness . . . Guess what?

"And since you were choosing people who you regarded as Master *Connectors,* what you told your partner were three ways YOU were a Master *Connector,* too.

"Surprise!"

Chris says with a booming laugh that fills the theater.

"Now, turn to the person sitting next to you or in front or behind. One of you go first and tell your partner three of the ways YOU are a Master *Connector.* Three qualities you admired so much in another Master *Connector* that you now know you have yourself.

"Start now, please," Chris instructs and walks up the side stairs on to the stage.

Chris gives them time to share, calling out for them to switch in the middle so each person gets a turn. Then he says, "There's a promise I didn't make to you all in the beginning that I always keep—whether I tell you or not. It's that I won't ask you to do something I wouldn't do myself.

"So, in keeping with that promise while you all were telling each other three things about the Master *Connector* you admired, I was doing that, too, with my partner Bart. He's our Staff Team leader . . .

"And you know what . . . now would be a great time for everybody on the team to step out of the shadows and get a big round of acknowledgement for all you do for us."

The audience didn't need any more prompting than that. They erupt—and Chris joins them enthusiastically—in a thunderstorm of applause as smiling Team Members around the room wave and thank them.

"Great *connecting*," Chris replies as he scans the audience . . . Let's see where to do I begin, oh yes, I would like to share with you the qualities of my Master Connector. And I'll start by saying a few things about him.

"I went on a witch hunt," Chris says, "and my Master *Connector* was the witch."

"My crusade, as I saw it, was to unmask this guy as a fraud—misguided and misguiding—and do all in my power to discredit him.

"I'll give you the punch line now: I failed miserably. Instead of bringing him crashing down, *he* raised *me* up. The man changed my life.

"I was 24 year's old and just beginning my ministry. I'd taken a position pastoring at The Real Life Church of God. It used to be called Hillcrest Church of God—a big, vibrant church with 700 people attending services, but . . . things had changed.

"The church I walked into was all broken windows and busted pews. No heat. Paint peeling. Outside, overgrown everything. And the congregation . . . It now consisted of 12 people. Average age, 76.

"Christians call the church 'the Body of Christ.' At Real Life Church, our Lord's body was in sorry shape. And my young pastor's dream became an instant nightmare.

"The only bright spot (for our church) was a young couple who'd just come to us from California. The woman was in her early 60s, and he was 45. Her mother came to our church. They were financially successful, and immediately became our largest tithers. I'd been to pastor school, so I knew that these were the people I had to *connect* with, so I did. We got to know, like and trust each other.

"I learned they were deeply into the self-help and personal development world."

"They told me I reminded them of the man they were following. They spoke about 'Living with Passion,' and 'Awakening the Giant Within.' I knew right away this guy was some kind of New Age guru. Fear of loss grabbed me in my ample gut. I believed I had to save these people from this dangerous charlatan and all his non-Christian crap.

"And I got my chance right away.

"The couple invited me to go to an event they were attending down in Florida. They'd pay for me. 'Yes!' I said 'Yes!' This self-help world of theirs was toast! I would expose the frauds an' phonies I knew them all to be and lock this couple into my church—and they were paying the way for my crusade. Perfect!

"First thing, I walk into the event and the music is rocking and loud, and people are clapping with the beat, and some are dancin' in the aisles. Sodom and Gomorrah. I knew it!

"Then this 6' 8" giant comes on stage and the place goes nuts. I'm thinkin' where's the Kool Aid! This is a cult. I knew it!

"He's rockin' around like everybody else. Then he spreads his arms wide like he's gathering up the energy in the room and throws it back on the audience with a big 'Oooooo YES!', and they go even more nuts.

"Jim Jones. Charles Manson. David Koresh. I knew it!"

"But . . . there was something else . . . something totally unexpected. Doubt entered my mind. I knew this was different. The guy on stage was different. So . . .

"The first thing out of the man's mouth, puts me into a Roddy Rowdy Piper sleeper hold.

"He said . . .

He was NOT a motivational speaker. He was NOT a guru. He said, "I'm the *Why Guy*."

"Wait. What? The *Why Guy* . . . I sat there. Mouth shut. Head empty. An odd feeling in the center of my chest.

"Like an alcoholic who knows he's just gotten sober by the Grace of God, that's how it felt.

"For the rest of the event, I was blown away. And blown away. And then blown away again. That guy and those people expressed—and I experienced—unconditional love for everyone. That had never happened to me in my life before. Ever!

"He had no preconceived ideas about the people he spoke with. No judgements of right/wrong, good/bad.

"He was totally present with all of us—every individual and the entire group. And he was the best listener I've ever experienced in my life.

"Oh, and passionate! *Everything* he did and said was filled with and overflowing with passionate energy. This is a man who literally *Lives With Passion*. Always and in all ways.

"I did say I was blown away—yes?" Chris asked with a laugh.

"When the student is ready . . .

"Well, that week I was ready and the teacher appeared. And he's been there—here," he said pointing to his heart, "ever since.

"It may surprise you—it absolutely surprises me—that I do not remember many to any details about that first event." Chris says. "I guess that's because all the big picture stuff just washed them out. I was transformed.

"'*Do not be conformed to this world with its superficial values and customs,*' the preacher said, '*but be transformed by the renewing of your mind.*'

> **"The Holy Spirit had begun the process of renewing my mind *and* my heart."**

"I believed then and now, that God sent me to that event at that time to renew my mind by demonstrating what Jesus Christ was all about—and to do it through this man's heart. Like King David, he had a heart for God and for everyone at that event.

"I came back home to my little dilapidated church and its doting congregation, and I was on fire! We turned the place and its people inside-out and down-side up. Extreme Church Makeover, no lie.

"And we did a make-over with the people in the church, too.

"Remember I said one thing I admired about the event was the 'fun' we had. Christians talk lots about 'joy,' but not much about fun. And have you ever had fun without joy?

"So, we started right away having fun. High-energy music when you walked into Sunday service. Heart-to-heart hugs all around—and these were people in their 70s and 80s who only ever hugged their grandkids. Now they were hugging me. Joy to the world! Absolutely.

> **"The church grew and grew. We got better and bigger in giant leaps and bounds."**

"Then a man named Wes Harden appeared. He had a youth group, and he wanted me to be the pastor. Now, I'm pretty good with grownups, but I'm *great* with kids. I jumped at the chance.

"And I jumped into double the salary, and the leather seats of a new Range Rover with an expense account, too.

"Starting with just 36 kids, we grew that youth ministry into more than 1,500 kids (plus another 100 adults). It was the largest youth group in the nation at the time. We had people flying in from around the world to see what we were doing, because it was such a phenomenon.

"And what we were doing brings me around to the two other things I admired most about that life-changing event: Fixing and Family.

"First off, I learned you never-ever try to 'fix' anybody. No one can ever feel love or have a true *connection* with you as long as they feel they're being fixed. Sure people, especially teenagers—can be broken. Life—even a young life—ain't easy. But when you approach people with the intent of *fixing* us, we shut down automatically. There's a better way.

"Remember I told you that speaker said he was 'the Why Guy.' That because a cornerstone of their approach is to help people understand *why* they thought and felt the things they did. Unlike my religious upbringing where one man got up and ranted about all the rules and regulations we had to live by, that event I went to showed people how to get a handle on their own why and how to handle and respond to our problems as opportunities. When you have that perspective, you see ALL your problems are *DISconnects* in one way or another—and all your opportunities are *connections* and *reconnections*.

"And speaking of *connections* and *reconnections*. Abby," Chris calls out. "Where are you?"

Abby stands and waves. "Here."

"Lioness, we have some unfinished business. Are you willing and able to continue our *connection*?" Chris is already coming down off the stage as Abby answers yes.

"Give Abby a big hand," Chris says as he walks up the aisle to stand next to her.

"Abby, when we last spoke—before you decided to take over my event by asking people to applaud for me," Chris has put his arm around Abby's shoulders and gives her a half hug and a smile.

"When last we spoke, you told me that one thought you had back on that day was that your mom didn't love you. That she wouldn't have yelled at you like she did if she did. Yes?"

"Yes," Abby says.

"You also said that your dad would not have left you all if he loved you."

"Yes on that one, too?"

"Yes. That one, too." Abby says.

"Abby are your parents still living?"

"Yes, they are."

"How often do you *connect* with them?"

"Well . . . " Abby says, letting her breath out with a sigh. "I see—*connect*—with my mom pretty much every month. My dad . . . not so much. I speak with my mom on the phone once a week or more. We're pretty good friends."

"You said you don't see—with your dad much. How much?"

"Five or six times a year. Maybe. He comes to the city once and a while, but mostly he comes over to my mom's when I'm visiting her, and that's when I see him."

"You told us that your mom and dad divorced not long after your brother—Tommy, right?—was born."

"No. My dad moved out. They never divorced. They just didn't live together."

"*That's* unusual," Chris says. "Reminds me of my parents. Girl, we *do* have quite a *connection*. Will you tell me about that: They don't live together, but they're still married?"

"My dad is a by-the-book Christian. He really wanted to be a minister more than anything, but he had to work all through high school to take care of his mother. His father died when he was two. He was her only child, and her health was always really bad, so he could never get to college. He's always had two jobs. Sometimes three."

"Anyway, he believed that divorce and abandoning your family wasn't the right thing, the Christian thing, to do, so . . . "

"So . . . " Chris picks up when Abby pauses, " although he didn't live with you and your brother and mother, he took care of y'all?"

"He did. He lived with his mother—she was an invalid and couldn't work, couldn't walk—and he took care of her until she died."

"Wow." Chris exclaims. "So your father was super committed to his faith *and* to taking care of your mom *and* you *and* your brother *and* his mom."

It isn't a question. Chris and Abby just stand looking into each other's eyes.

"So your Dad . . . What's his name?"

"Arthur. Art," Abby tells Chris.

"So Art gave up on his dream of being a minister to care for his mother, like his father would have done had he been alive. Worked two, sometimes three jobs to support two families. Stayed married to your mom and was always around when you were growing up . . . *And* argued with your mom about money a lot. Have I got all that right?"

"Yup."

"I take it your mom didn't work while you were growing up?" Chris asks.

"He wouldn't let her," Abby says. "He wanted her to be with her children all the time."

"Abby, I assume you grew up a Christian, yes?"

"I did," Abby says.

"Do you recall Jesus telling His disciples the night before he died, 'Greater love hath no man than this, that he lay down his life for his friends'?"

Abby nods.

"Looking at your dad, at how he lived his life and what was important to him, does it make any sense for you that he laid down a bunch of *parts* of his life for his friends—for you and his family?"

Abby nods again, and this time there are tears in her eyes.

"Did you know your grandmother well—you dad's mom?"

"Not really. I mean, we saw her a bunch, but she was real quiet. I think she was in pain a lot."

"So you and Tommy didn't sit on her lap, have her read to you, or snuggle much?"

"No."

"Did she ever tell you she loved you?"

"No. Never."

"Did she tell your dad?"

Abby is thoughtful, then says, "I don't remember her saying 'I love you' to any of us."

"Did your dad tell you he loved you Abby?"

"I don't remember."

"Try," Chris encourages her, and repeats: "Did your dad tell you he loved you Abby?"

"No. Not much,' she replies, and the tears have started flowing fully now.

Chris bends down and puts his arms around Abby. She melts into him and cries her heart out.

After a good bit, Abby steps back and uses the tissue she is offered to dry her eyes and blow her nose.

"So, Abby," Chris says, looking gently down at her *connecting* in a way the entire room could feel, "You said that if your dad really loved you he wouldn't have left. Do you think that's true?"

"No. Not now."

"And Abby, do you tell your dad that you love him?"

"No," she says, taking in a big sniffling breath of air. "No, I don't. And I know I should."

"Do you love him?" Chris asks.

"Oh yes. Yes, I do!" Abby says with power and great conviction.

About four or five rows down the aisle from where Chris and Abby are standing, a man stands up and takes a step towards them. He must have changed his mind, because he turns and sits back down. Out of the corner of his eye Chris notices immediately.

"Excuse me Abby," he says, putting a hand on her shoulder, and walks down the aisle to stand next to the man who had gotten up and sat back down.

"You okay?" Chris asks.

The man—probably in his 50s or 60s, silvering hair neatly trimmed, wearing a suit, his white shirt collar was open and his tie is stuck in this breast pocket—stands up.

"I'm not sure," the man says. "Well . . . no . . . I'm not okay. I mean, I'm okay, but . . . "

His cheeks are ruddy. His nose and the area under his eyes are red and puffy. There are traces of tears.

"Will you tell me about what's going on for you?" Chris asks.

"Sure," the man says, and he reaches out to shake Chris's hand and introduces himself, "I'm Adrian Schwartz."

"Good to meet you Adrian," Chris returns his hand shake. "I'm Chris Dorrity. How can I help you Adrian?"

"You already have."

"Good!" Chris exclaims. "That's my job."

"Adrian, you stood up a minute ago and looked like you were coming up the aisle, but the you sat back down. What was happening then?"

"I'm not sure. I was sitting there listening to you and Abby. And as I listened it was like this fog came around me. Everybody else in the theater disappeared. I was just sitting there. Isolated. Alone. I could hear you. But it was like . . . I dunno.' Weird. That's never happened to me before."

"Were you having any specific thoughts or feelings when that happened?" Chris asks.

"I have an Abby of my own," Adrian says, and as he does, he lets out a deep sigh. "Close to the same age I suspect. We haven't spoken in a long time. She doesn't like me very much."

"Really. What makes you say that Adrian?"

"We're not close. We've never been close. As I listened to Abby, I realized that I was much like her dad. I've worked my whole life. I didn't want my wife and child to grow up as I did, so I worked to give them everything I didn't have. And I did. Except . . ."

"Except?" Chris repeats back to Adrian as a question.

"Except me. I gave my business all my time. Not my wife or daughter. My only daughter. Only child."

"Regrets. I've had a lot. But then again, too many to mention."

Chris plays with the lyrics of the Sinatra classic.

Adrian laughs. "Yeah. Like that," he says.

"Adrian, I've learned some things about how you and I operate. One big one is that we the people *always*—and I do mean *always and in all ways*—do what's most important to us. In the moment, every moment, we *always* do what's most important.

"When you were giving your business all your time, that was what was most important to you." Chris pauses and then asks Adrian, "Does that make sense?"

"I see that," he says.

"What was most important for you Adrian was providing for your family. Giving them a better life than you had. Yes?"

"Yes."

"So, Adrian, I want you to think about the *connection* you had with Abby's story?"

Adrian takes a deep sigh. "I didn't tell my daughter that I loved her. I *showed* her. Gave her the best of everything. I guess I thought that was enough."

"And just now, in the fog, you had second thoughts?" Chris asked and after a pause added, "And the love you feel for your daughter became what was most important to you?"

"Exactly," Adrian says with a very large sigh.

"Do you want to do anything about that?"

Adrian looks at Chris wide-eyed—another large sigh Then he looks down at his feet.

"I get a 'Yes, but . . . ' from you Adrian. Am I close?"

"Not close. Spot on," Adrian replies.

"What thoughts and feelings are you having right now?" Chris asks.

"Oh . . . the thought I have is my daughter won't care. As I said, she doesn't like me much."

"Do you like her?"

"Oh . . . " And Adrian is clearly a bit shocked by the question. "Boy . . . I don't want to say this, but . . . no."

"Ah . . . So you're human."

Adrian looks at Chris, his face a big question mark.

"Adrian, let me see if you're like I am here. I like people who like me. I *love* people who love me. And I really can't stand people who don't like me at all."

Adrian laughed. "We are *connected*," he says.

"So, Adrian, do you love your daughter? What's her name?"

"Karen. Of course I do."

"Adrian, you know, unconditional love is lots easier than unconditional like."

Adrian laughs again.

"So, back to my question: Do you want to do anything about that? Is that what's most important to you now?"

Adrian takes a deep breath, and as he does, he stands taller. "I do . . . It is." He says.

"And is there still a 'but' there?"

"Ah . . . nervous. Scared. I don't really know how."

"Practice makes perfect," Chris says and turns to look back up the aisle. "Lioness, would you be willing to help Adrian out here?"

Abby says sure, and Chris asks her to come down and stand with him and Adrian. He introduces them to each other, and Adrian, true to form, sticks out his hand.

"Hang on," Chris says. "Adrian, would I be correct in saying you ain't the hugging type?"

Adrian laughs and blushes, and Chris says, "Thought as much. So, Abby, would it be okay with you to give and take a heart-to-heart hug with Adrian? You can be his hug coach."

Abby doesn't wait a moment. She moves over to Adrian and puts her arms around his shoulders, heart-to-heart.

Adrian hesitates a second and then with a deep sigh of relief, his eyes closed, gives himself fully to receiving and returning Abby's hug.

Chris turns to the audience and spreads his arms, but before he can say a word, people are on their feet cheering with applause.

"So, Adrian, just now, when you and your hugging coach were doing your thing, did you feel anything?"

"Yes."

"Okay, a multiple choice question, Adrian. Was the feeling you experienced A. Love. B. Love. C. Love. Or D. All of the above."

Adrian laughs. Large and freely. "D. The love *connection*," he says, and everybody laughs at that.

"Adrian, just for practice, are you willing and able to say 'I love you' to Abby as if she were your daughter Karen?"

Without hesitation Adrian says, "Abby, I love you."

After a brief pause to collect himself he says, "Karen, I love you."

The audience erupts with spontaneous applause.

"Adrian, I've got an idea. Do you have a phone, and do you know your daughter's number?"

"I do . . . and I do," he says.

"Are you up for giving Karen a call and telling her that you love her?"

"Whoa! Ah . . . Okay. Yes, I am."

"Need any moral support?" Chris asks, and before Adrian can respond, Abby takes his arm and says, "Will you let me help you?"

The smile on Adrian's face goes beyond ear-to-ear.

"Yes. Absolutely. Thank you."

"Question for you all," Chris says to the audience. "Anybody else have a call they want to make right now?"

More hands go up than can be counted.

With his biggest smile of the day, Chris says, "Folks, it's a bit early for the dinner break, but . . . since so many of you have some *connecting* to do, let's take it now—and make it longer than usual.

"Before you go, as you make your calls I'm asking you to keep in heart and mind one of the things I said I admired most: not fixing.

"You may have the thought that you're going to *fix* your Relationship—and I understand that it may indeed look broken to you.

"I'm asking you to set that thought aside and focus on one thing and one thing only today: *Connecting*. Heart-to-heart. Just *connect*. With your head and your heart. Words and music. Reach out with, as Adrian said, *the love connection*.

"And one more thing. I'm asking you to set one thing aside, and believe me when I tell you there's no greater assassin of *connection*. It's a born killer. You have GOT TO LET GO OF . . . "

"RESENTMENT"

"Resentments are sneaky little devils. They can convince us they're justified, that we're right, and the other person is wrong. They cripple our hearts. Vandalize our happiness. Sabotage our love. Like I said, they're the assassins of *connection*.

"Most of us have been on the receiving end of an injustice at some time in our lives. Most of us know someone who's complained of an injustice we've done to him or her. Life can be a breeding ground for resentments—if we let it be.

"Yeah, but this time I really was wronged.

"Maybe so. But holding on to resentment isn't the solution. And sadly for some of us our resentment list resembles the Atlanta phone directory. Deal with your hurt and harmed feelings. Learn whatever lesson is at hand. Then let those feelings go.

"The key is in the word itself," Chris explained. "The *sentment* part is just like 'sentiment' and 'sentimental,' and they both come from the Latin *sentire,* meaning *to feel.* 'Re' means over again, like a do-over. So re-sentment is to feel—and it's always a bad feeling—over again.

"That's what we do with resentment. Something bad happens and we react with a negative feeling. And that would be okay if we just moved on, but we don't. We re-experience those same bad feelings again and again and over again. So, instead of having that one feel-bad moment, we have it hundreds, even thousands of times.

"Can you see why I said there's no greater assassin of *connection* than resentment?" Chris asks the audience. "Why it's such a born *connection* killer?

"The problem is, no matter whom we're resenting, the upset is ultimately directed against ourselves. It's as Nelson Mandela said, 'Resentment is like drinking poison and then hoping it will kill your enemies.'

"Take a moment right now. Search your heart. Have you tricked yourself into harboring resentment for the person you'd like to call tonight?

"If you have, take another moment and let that resentment go—as best you can. Hey look, you made it up to begin with. It's not true, and it's not false. It's just something you made up. **Let it go!**

"And look," Chris adds. "You may have to let it go, and then let it go again, and again 'cause it comes right back. Takes practice. Makes progress."

"CONNECT . . . OR DIE," Chris says.

"So, anybody got a call to make?" And, as the audience starts out of their seats, he shouts, "HEY! HEY! HEY! Have fun out there! That's mandatory. Okay?"

He looks at his watch, announces the break would be one-hour and 59 minutes, the music comes on immediately, and people are literally jumping out of their seats and running out of the theater, phones in hand.

They're Baaack . . .

Do you have any idea what it must take to have 1,500 individuals—especially people who were so excited and jacked-up they were bouncing off the walls—all be back in the theater and in their seats on time? Clearly, Chris and his staff know what they are doing.

As further testament of that fact, the volume of the expected boisterous party music is down a click or two. But those diminished decibels aren't noticed at all, because it is more than compensated for—actually *over*-compensated for—by extra-loud, crowd hugging, high-fiving, sharing, and shouting back and forth.

People are clearly *connecting* with each other at a whole new level now.

Shouting over the din of the audience, Chris asks loudly from the stage, "How do you feel?"

In return, "Great! Awesome! Fantastic," and many more high-energy exclamations are yelled back at him.

"Now, let me guess," he says. "A bunch of you did some great *connecting* on your dinner break. Raise your hand if you made a *connection*—or a *REconnection*—with someone important to you in your life?"

Hands up galore.

"Great!" Chris says. "Now, I want you to share with the person next to you—or in front or behind, or across the aisle—what was the best thing about making that *connection,* for you, and what made that best thing the best thing. What was so special about making that *connection* for you? Make sure you both get a chance to share. You'll have plenty of time.

"And," Chris adds, "for any of you who weren't able to *connect* with the person you wanted to reach, not to worry. Tell your partner who it was you wanted to *connect* with, and what you were wanting to tell them—and be sure to say what makes telling them that important to you when you are able to *connect* with them.

"Do that now, please.

"And remember . . . " Chris instructs as people begin to share, "Stop, Look, and Listen. Be wide open and *coo-nnn-eee-cccc-ttt* with your partner heart-to-heart. Both words *and* music.

"Go!"

If the noise in the room had been loud before, that was nothing compared to the sound the people start making now.

Like a touchdown celebration at the Super Bowl. You could not have heard a bomb drop.

After about three minutes or so, Chris tells them to switch and make sure they both get to be heard.

In another three minutes, he says—rather he shouts as loud as he can (because that was the only way he could be heard)—"Aw right! Now, find a new partner, someone you haven't *connected* with yet today. Get up and find them and share again the best thing about your phone *connection* over dinner and what made that so great. Do that now, please!"

After people have shared with their second partners, Chris has them pick another new third partner and share their *connection* once again.

The scene is amazing to observe. Throughout this whole process, the energy in the room doesn't diminish one bit. If anything, it just keeps increasing.

Expecting it would take more than shouting to get everybody's attention this time, Chris has a big graphic appear on the stage screen along with the 'Boom. Boom. Boom' of a big bass drum.

As the image appears and the drum stops beating, Chris shouts, "Stop! Stop! S-T-O-P Stop!"

It takes a bit, but the smiling, happy people in the theater make their way back to their seats and settle down.

Even though some folks are still talking back and forth, Chris says, "Okay, we're going to hear from a number of you about what you were sharing with your partners. But I'm going to give this exercise a unique little twist.

"Think of it like '*Connection's* Greatest Hits, Volume One.' Did any of *your partners* share an experience of *connecting* with you that just blew you away!?!

"Who just heard about an *extraordinary, awesome, amazing connection* your partner had over dinner!?!"

If you had expected just a few hands here and there to go up, you would have been very surprised. It truly seems like more than half the people in the theater have their hands up, most of them waving excitedly like a third grader who knows the right answer.

"Wow!" Chris exclaims. "I've never seen so many hands go up like this before. Y'all ARE *Awesome!* No kidding. You are the best group ever!"

He points to a woman on the aisle about half way up. "Dear lady . . . In the great looking green jacket. Please, stand and tell us your name."

Miriam stands, but before she gets her name out, the theater erupts with resounding applause.

"I want to nominate Paige," she says as the ovation faded.

"*Beecaauuse . . .* " Chris asks, drawing the word out playfully.

"*Beecaauuse . . .* " Miriam starts, mimicking Chris, but abruptly stops. "Don't you want her to tell you what happened?" she asks.

"Nope," Chris says. "You tell me, Miriam. But first, Paige, where are you? Will you stand, please?" And she did to more thunder-claps of applause.

"Okay," Miriam begins. "Well, it was just so cool. Paige hasn't spoken with her brother in years. Four years, is that right?" she asked looking over at Paige, who nods to her.

You see, her brother was a drug addict, and she just couldn't stand watching him struggle and suffer. He was self-destructing, and she didn't want to watch him go down the tubes."

"She told me she'd felt betrayed by her brother. That before the drugs, they'd been so close, such great friends, but he'd pulled away. He became isolated. He left her. He left everybody.

"Before Paige called him, she told me that here, today, she'd realized that it wasn't her brother that was doing the *DISconnecting*. She was. She *DISconnected* FROM him. *She'd* pulled away from him. *She* became isolated, too. She saw that in reality *she left him*.

"And she told me she realized that she was punishing him.

"She was hurt and angry, and she got back at him by withholding her *connection* with him. And when Paige told me that, . . . she broke down and started to cry."

As she tells the story of Paige's realizations, Miriam starts to cry as well. So does Paige and a number of folks in the audience. Even Chris wipes his eyes.

"Forgiveness," Chris says gently, "is giving up your right to punish."

"Go on, please."

"Well," Miriam continues, breathing back a sniffle, "I just gave her a big heart-to-heart hug. I asked if she was okay and asked if she was good to call and *connect* with her brother?

"You should have seen her, Chris. She got this determined look on her face, pulled out her phone like it was a six-gun or something, and dialed—punching the numbers from memory!

"When I heard her say, 'Hey, little brother, it's Paige,' I just stood next to her, ready to be there for her if she needed me. But she didn't.

"In only seconds, she was telling her brother how sorry she was that she'd *DISconnected* from him. That she wasn't there for him when she could have been, should have been. Then she asked, 'Please, can we get *REconnected?*' She wanted to know what she *could* do to make things right between them.

"Chris," Miriam says, "I just stood there in awe I felt so much respect and admiration for Paige. She was so strong. So willing to accept responsibility. To be vulnerable. I just . . . I just fell in love with her right then and there.

"But wait . . . " Miriam says, pausing to wipe her nose with a tissue. "That's not the best part. Can I let Paige tell you the rest herself?"

Chris is nodding his head up and down and smiling. After a long breath out from deep down and a quick 'Thanks, God' looking up at the ceiling, he says, "Sure. Paige, you up for that?"

She says "Sure," too, and begins, "Buddy told me that he'd been clean for nine months. He says now he knows what it was like to be pregnant," Paige laughs.

"He told me he got into a 12-step program. And he was on Step 9, which he explained was where you call people up and make amends to them for the wrongs you've done—the pain you caused them while you were drugging and drinking.

"He told me that he'd already called a bunch of people to make amends, but he said they were just practice sessions. That *I* was the person he wanted to speak with the most. He told me he'd set the calendar alarm on his phone a week ago for 10:30 *tomorrow morning* to *call me* and make his amends.

"And then—and this is perfect, Buddy," Paige says with a big grin over-taking her face, "He said, "Paige, I love you, but damnit sis, you always spoil everything! I'm calling you tomorrow to make amends after all these years, but nooooo. You've got to call *ME* first, so *YOU* can make amends to *ME!*"

If Paige has more to say, she doesn't get the chance because 1,500 people are on their feet applauding, cheering, and high-fiving each other, all celebrating Paige and the awesome power of her *connection.*

After all his years of teaching, preaching—and often screeching—about *connection,* it's got to be really hard for Chris Dorrity to be blown away, but he is. He just keeps nodding his head, like one of those bobblehead dolls, saying "Wow. Wow. Wow. Wow." Over and over again.

Chris gathers himself, takes one of his huge deep breaths, and says, "Folks, you ARE the most amazing group of people I have ever had the honor to be with. You've all come so far, so fast. Y'all truly blow me away."

Another big breath and Chris says, "Okay. I'm throwing away the playbook. You guys are so awesome, so head-felt and heart-smart, I'm going to trust you with something I've wanted to do before, but always held back on.

"I'm asking for any folks who did NOT make the *connection* they'd hoped for over the break . . .

"Any of you who reached out . . . You called . . . You tried . . . Gave it your best shot, but it didn't go the way you wanted.

"I talking to any of you who are sitting there right now . . .

"Thinking and feeling discouraged, disheartened, disappointed you didn't *connect*."

"If that's you, I'm asking you to get up, right now and make your way to stand in the nearest aisle."

Thirty-two people get up and make their way to stand in the two aisles. One of them, is Adrian.

"Oh my!" Chris exclaims. "Adrian."

"Adrian, will you please come up here and sit next to me. I want to speak with you, but first we've got some things to do."

As Adrian makes his way to the stage to sit with Chris, Chris speaks to the group.

"My friends, there are 31 people standing in the aisles. Stop and look at them, please.

"Now, you know it took real courage for every one of them to get up from their safe seats and stand in the aisle for all of us to see.

"These brave men and women swallowed their pride, set their egos aside, and were willing to be open, accepting, and, most of all, *vulnerable* in front of 1,500 people."

As he speaks, Chris puts both his hands out, palms up in a gesture of STOP. "The perfect time for a great round of applause to acknowledge these folks, I know, but hold on to that for the moment.

"These folks wanted to *connect* with someone who was very important to them in their life, but they didn't. Doesn't take a lot of smarts to guess that each of these men and women see themselves as having failed. And another guess . . . They all feel pretty darn *DISconnected* right now."

Chris scans the entire audience, laser-looking at every one in the theater.

"Ladies and gentlemen, as of this moment, I am no longer leading this conference. You are."

"I pass the baton over to you. Each and every one of you. You're the leaders now.

"These people standing up in the aisles are the tops of the Hawaiian Alps. They're your brothers and sisters, maybe your mom or your dad or your kids.

"They need something from you right now. I think what they each need is an authentic heart-to-heart *connection* with y'all.

"But . . . " Chris adds, "like I said, I'm not in charge anymore. You are. You're leading this conference. Not me.

"So what are you going to do about them?"

Immediately, dozens of people shoot from their seats and go right to the nearest person standing in the aisles and hug them. Then, those first dozen heart-to-heart huggers are quickly followed by dozens more, and then dozens more, and then not one seat in the theater is taken.

The aisles are jammed. Overflowing with people waiting to hug and be hugged. Laughing. Crying. *Connecting.*

A good guess would be not one of those 1,500 people have ever experienced anything like this before. It was like Times

Square the day that WWII ended. All that was missing was the ticker tape confetti.

Chris sits calmly on the stage looking over the remarkable scene with a big, contented smile. Adrian is sitting next to him. Smiling, too, and Chris has his arm around Adrian's shoulder.

The room is abuzz and ablaze with energy for at least a half-an-hour, probably lots more. Nobody is keeping time. Clearly Chris isn't. He sits on stage fully focused on speaking and listening in animated conversation about who-knows-what with Adrian.

Eventually, as people begin returning to their seats, Chris stands up and walks to the very front center edge of the stage.

"Okay," he begins, "with your permission I'm going to take back my conference. He laughs as he speaks.

"I'm not going to ask you how that was like for y'all. I have a rule I call DMA. It stands for Don't Make Assumptions. So, although I'm pretty sure I've got a great sense of the size and shape of your *connections* just now, I want this unique experience to be a gift you got and gave for yourself. I trust—fully and completely—it was as special for you as it was for me.

"Just watching you, Adrian and I were blown way away!"

"And speaking of Adrian," Chris says turning back and going to sit next to him, "ladies and gentlemen, give it up for the one, the only . . . *Adrian!*" And they do.

When the applause subsides and people sit back down, Chris begins speaking with Adrian.

"So, my friend, I was surprised to see you standing in the aisle with the people who didn't *connect*. Did you reach Karen? Did you speak with her?"

"I did," Adrian replies, and the room is immediately filled with something best described as uneasy expectation. Adrian's energy has shifted immediately and is clearly leaking away.

"Okay, are you willing and able to share with me—with us—about it?"

"Adrian looks up at the ceiling and takes a deep breath before answering. "Sure," he says.

"Adrian, I want you to be like a newspaper reporter with me here. Journalism 101. Focus on 'just the facts.' Who. What. Where. When. And let *why* come later.

"And folks," Chris says, "in all your conversations for *connection*, please avoid asking *Why?*"

"Remember when as a kid your parents or teachers asked you, 'Why did you do this . . . Say that . . . think this?' Made you defensive right away, didn't it?

"We all *remember* experiencing that, and so even as adults when someone asks us 'why?' we automatically look for an explanation, a reason, an excuse. It's natural. But it's an immediate *DISconnect*.

"*What* questions are way better. We don't take them personally. And it's even better," Chris explains, "to begin with, '*Help me understand* how you chose to do that . . . say this . . . think that way about this or that.

"Can you see the difference?" Chris asks. All the nodding heads and yeses from the audience show that they do.

"So, Adrian, help me understand what happened for you?"

"Well," Adrian begins, "Who was Karen. What was my call with her. Where was outside in the courtyard. When was over the dinner break." He looks over at Chris with a smile.

Chris smiles back. "Clever man," he says.

"So, you *connected* with Karen?"

"I did. It took a while for me to muster up the courage to call, but I did."

"Aaannnddd . . . ?" Chris asks.

"And we talked. She didn't recognize my voice at first. That felt weird. She asked, 'Who's this?' and when I said, 'It's your dad,' there was a long silence. Also pretty weird. Then she said, 'Dad . . . Ummmm. What do you want?' And that was weirder still."

"Kind of took the wind out of your sails, huh?" Chris asks.

"Yeah, it did."

"'What I *need* Karen,' I told her, 'is to tell you I'm sorry. All the time you were growing up I wasn't really there for you. I mean, I was *there,* but I wasn't really *there.* We didn't really get to know each other. That's my fault, and I'm truly sorry.'"

There is silence in the theater. Chris just looks at Adrian, and you could feel his full attention on him. His face is expressionless, but Chris's *connection* with Adrian was heart-to-heart, and everybody in the place could feel it.

Adrian breaks the silence. "I told Karen that I loved her. I told her that I hoped we could make a fresh start. I told her I was sorry. I said that a number of times."

"Okay, so at this point in the call Adrian, where is the focus?" Chris asks directly. "Is it on Karen—or on you?"

"Oh wow," Adrian says. "On me. It was all about me."

"Yup," Chris says. "And what percent of the time on the call were you the one speaking Adrian—one to 100?"

"Ninety percent," Adrian replies. "Maybe more."

"Okay, so you got that one—yes?"

"Next time you can do more asking Karen about herself and listening.

"Now, tell me the good news. What was said—by either of you—that made you feel good, Adrian?"

"We did speak about the last time we were together. It was years ago. We went to a pizza place. Her favorite. And there was one of those big glass boxes where you try to pick up a stuffed animal with this mechanical claw, and I tried to win this bear for her. I dropped $22 on that game and didn't get her bear. We laughed about that.

"I told her she was my daughter, and that would never change. That she *was* my pride and joy. That all the time I spent working so hard and such long hours was to give her the best of everything and anything I could. I told her I knew how to do that, but what I didn't know was how to be her father. I told her I just didn't think she liked me . . .

> **"I said over and over again, 'I love you Karen,' but she never once said I love you back."**

"I reached out and *connected*, but . . . "

"But . . . ? "Chris asks after a long pause.

"But, I didn't really *connect*," Adrian says.

"Really?" Chris replies. "You spoke with her—yes? I mean, Karen didn't hang up on you, did she?"

"Yes, I spoke with her, and no, she didn't hang up."

"All right! Ten points for Gryffindor," Chris says with a laugh.

"Adrian, ever do any gardening?"

"No," Adrian replies.

"Okay, so you're not a farmer. But imagine for a moment that you are. You plant a carrot. Sun shines on it. You water it. Nourish the earth around it. And you come back in a week and pull it up to see how it's doing.

"How's that gonna' work for ya?"

Adrian laughs, and Chris laughs with him. "Not!" Adrian says.

"Adrian, you planted a seed today. And it was a super-*connection*-seed. An 'I love you' seed. They're the best. None better."

"How long has it been since you and Karen *connected*?"

"Way too long. I'm embarrassed to say."

"Years and years. Yes?" Chris asks.

". . . and years," Adrian adds.

"So, RELAX Adrian. Don't go pulling the *connection* with your Karen-carrot up to see how it's growing. Even our Creator rested on the seventh day—and, Adrian, you did some great creating today. Do you get that . . . ?"

Before Adrian could speak, a voice from the audience shouts out like a college cheerleader . . .

"I get it! We all get it!"

As Abby runs down the aisle and up on the stage the theater erupts, and magically so does the music, which gets everybody up on their feet and rocking out.

Abby is on stage with a microphone in hand a staff member handed her, and she rushes to heart-to-heart hug Chris first and then Adrian.

It is minutes before she lets Adrian go and steps back. The entire time the audience is hooting and hollering.

When the theater starts to quiet down, Chris says, "It looks like I'm about to give up control of my event for the second time tonight. No third! She's done this before," he said with a hearty laugh.

"Dear Abby," he says, "Adrian and all of these good people are in your hands," and he moves about six feet off standing to the side of Adrian and Abby.

"Adrian! I love you!" Abby shouts into the microphone, and people are on their feet cheering again.

Once again, the emotional high in the theater takes a while to calm down. Abby waits. When it does she begins to speak to Adrian.

"Adrian, I DO love you. Our *connection* has meant the world to me today. And *FOR* me.

"Look, I know some of what your daughter Karen may have been feeling today. When you grow up *DISconnected* with your father, that's all you know. You've got nothing to compare with, so you think that's what fathers and daughters do. That's just the way it is.

"So please, understand Karen's thoughts and feelings. You showed up for her today as someone she's never met before. She met her real father, maybe for the first time today. That's probably how she felt.

"And, if Karen is anything like me—and I'll bet she is—she's spent a lifetime plugging up the holes in her *DISconnected* relationship with you, so those empty, missing places didn't hurt so bad.

"Adrian, you've got to know that every little girl in the world wants love and affection from her dad. More than anything. And when we don't get that, we try to make it okay by covering up those needs—or filling them with something or someone else. To make it all okay, we talk ourselves into not caring anymore. We *DISconnect* big time. It's less painful that way.

"And, Adrian . . . " Abby stops and looks over at Chris, her eyes wide asking him if she should continue.

"Lioness, the moment you stop doing better than I could with Adrian, I'll take back the mic. You go, girl. You're doing awesome!"

With a big smile from ear to ear, Abby starts again.

"Adrian, today when you said, 'Abby, I love you.' You were my dad saying that to me. I actually heard my father's voice saying, 'I love you' to me. You planted a seed with Karen tonight, but you planted a five foot tall blue spruce sapling with me.

"As soon as I knew you'd connected on the phone with Karen, I walked off and called my dad. And I know you were disappointed with your *connection* with Karen, but my *connection* with my dad was over the freakin' moon!"

Abby says—or more accurately *cheers*—standing on one foot as she shoots her fist up in the air shouting "Yes! Yes! Yes!"

You can guess what happens next in the theater.

When the audience calms down, Abby continues.

"And Adrian, it's all your fault! And you, too, big guy," she says turning to Chris, who nods and bows like an actor accepting a curtain call with a sweeping gesture of his right arm.

"I couldn't have done it without you, Adrian. I know you guys keep talking about my courage, but I'll tell ya,' when I dialed my dad, more than my knees were shaking.

"I just kept replaying you saying to me, 'Abby, I love you. Abby, I love you. Abby, I love you.' When my dad answered the phone, I actually blew it and said out loud, 'Abby, I love you,' by mistake and then burst out laughing—and my dad did, too.

"We had the best *connection*– the best connection ever!"

"I thanked him for laying down his life for us. I told him I know now how very much he loved us all. That he may not have told us, but he sure showed us. Big time!

"The last thing I said to him on the call was this was the best day of my life. And here, look at this" (she says handing Adrian her phone. "He sent me this text."

"Adrian," Chris says, "Will you read it to us—if that's okay Abby?."

Abby nods and says, "Sure!" and Adrian reads the text.

"Abby, I LOVE YOU!" Adrian adds, "I LOVE YOU is in all caps. This was the best day of my life, too. Can we do it again tomorrow. (Smiley face.) Visit. Soon. Yes?"

When Adrian finishes reading, there are tears in his eyes. He throws his arms around Abby with a heart-to-heart hug that literally lights up the room. As if by magic, Celine Dion's *Because You Love Me* starts playing softly but clearly in the background.

And the staff is running out of tissues.

Chris walks over to Adrian and Abby, and they share a group hug.ABby, up on her toes, gives Chris a kiss on each cheek and says something in his ear nobody could hear. Adrian takes Chris's right hand in both of his and with a silent 'Thank you' on his lips gazes intently into Chris's eyes. Then, arm in arm, Abby and Adrian walk off the stage, down the stairs, and back to their seats.

Even after the applause quiets completely, Chris stands silently on the stage. Usually, when there's silence in a room filled with 1,500 people, it feels pretty uncomfortable for everybody. There isn't a trace of that here.. Just a peaceful, pervasive calm.

The entire theater has taken a deep breath and is smiling with contentment.

"You couldn't hear what Abby said to me," Chris eventually breaks the silence and speaks to the group. She told me . . .

> **"God brought us all here today
> and *connected* us together
> for a purpose."**

"I'm going to share a personal story" Chris says. "It's a *very* personal story for me, and it needs a DISCLAIMER . . .

"You're aware that I've been a Christian preacher and a pastor, and this is a story about Jesus Christ. I am *absolutely* a zealous advocate for my faith, but I am *absolutely NOT* attempting to convert you here. I want to have that be very clear and clean for you all."

Chris pauses and scans the theater.

"Jesus Christ is called 'the Son of Man' and 'the Son of God.' More than a human son whose DNA, genes and ancestry carry part of his father within him, for in Christianity, God the Father and God the Son are two aspects of one and the same Creator. Father and Son inseparable throughout eternity. They've always been *connected*.

> **"Understanding this divine *connection*
> between the Father and the Son
> is what's important here."**

"Jesus was all and always about His *connection* with His Father God—and Their *connection* with all of us. Everything Christ did and said came from His *connection* with His Father.

"'... I pray for those who will believe in me through their message, that all of them may be one, Father, just as you are in me and I am in you ... I have given them the glory that you gave me, that they may be one as we are one—I in them and you in me ...'

"Adrian!" Chris shouts out. "How's that for a *love connection?*"

"Amen," Adrian calls back with a broad smile.

"Any kidding aside," Chris says, "*connection* begins in your heart. The source of all *connection* is love.

"If you know the story, you know that Jesus sacrificed his life on the cross for the salvation of all humanity. He taught us, '*Greater love hath no man than this, to lay down his life for his friends,*' and that's what He did at Calvary.

"But for me ... He did something more. Even greater than enduring the *extra*ordinary pain and suffering of giving up his *earthly* life for our sins.

"Shortly before his death he cried out, '*Eli, Eli, lema sabachthani?*' '*My God, my God, why have you forsaken me?*'

"*Forsaken* me," Chris repeats and pauses over the word.

"*Forsaken,*" he repeats again. "Abandoned. Deserted. Renounced.

"My God, my God, why have you *DISconnected* from me?"

"For the first time in His eternal existence Jesus gave up, severed, lost, His *connection* to His Father God. His *love connection* . . . His *love connection* with the very Source of love itself.

"When I looked at the crucifixion from that perspective, I saw the inconceivable sacrifice Christ made for us—for me—my sense of the precious value, awesome power, and eternal importance of *Connection* overwhelmed me completely.

"And the thought I was left with was . . .

"CONNECT . . . OR DIE."

Again, Chris is silent as is the audience. Very, very silent.

"I'm going to recommend something to you," Chris says. "It's not required—although for me it's more than mandatory. So be open to it. Consider this please.

"I believe that THE most important *connection* for each and every one of us is our *connection* to God—however and whatever way you understand God to be in your life. The *connection* to your Source. Your higher power. Your Creator. Your essential *Love Connection*.

"C. S. Lewis wrote, 'A car is made to run on gasoline, and it would not run properly on anything else. Now God designed the human machine to run on Himself. He Himself is the fuel our spirits were designed to burn, or the food our spirits were designed to feed on. There is no other.'

"Our *Connection* to our Creator is THE most important *Connection* of all."

"There's much more I can say, and want to say about this, but I'm going to let it be for now. After all, it is almost 1:00 in the morning. If you want to talk more about that sometime, let me know.

"So . . . " Chris takes a deep breath before continuing.

"Throughout our time together here you've gotten a triple-dose of the importance and power—and necessity—of CONNECTION in all our lives.

"I believe with all my heart and soul that *connection* is THE solution to any and every challenge and problem we face in the world today.

"And the thing is—the *crazy thing is*—we are all already and always *connected!*

"So . . . " Chris asks, "What's up—or down—with that?

"What's gone down is . . . that we forgot.

"And when you forget something, what is there to do?" Chris answered his own question, "Remember.

"That's it. That's all. Just *remember.* Your *CONNECTION.*"

"I'm going to have you do something with me right now. It's an exercise you can do anywhere, anytime that centers you, focuses you, empowers you.

"I'll demonstrate what I'll be having you do.

"Raise both hands up over your head, reaching for the sky. As high as you can, stretching without stress. And as you raise your hands take a deep breath in. Fill yourself up completely. Like this . . . "

And Chris demonstrates raising both hands, stretching as high as he could and taking a deep breath in at the same time. With his hands still way up in the air, he instructs the group, "Now, when I tell you, bring your arms down, fast, and as you do blow all the air inside you out through your nose." And he demonstrates that.

"You got it?" And he shows them again as he tells them again. "Hands way up, deep breath in, arms down fast, exhaling explosively out your nose.

"Good. You *are* so good!

"I'm going to have you do that 7 times in all. When we're done, sit quietly, with your eyes closed, and just relax. I'll tell you what to do from there. Okay?

"All right," Chris says. "Sit with your back straight. Close your eyes if you want to. Let's begin.

"Arms up, way up and breath in!" Everyone in the theater follows along.

"Great! Now, pull your arms down, fast, and breathe out like an explosion through your nose." Again, everyone in the theater follows along.

"Perfect! Okay, again. Arms way up, reach for the sky and breath in!" And after a two second pause, Chris continues. "Now, pull your arms down, fast, and breathe out strong. Every bit out.

"Yes! Great job. Again. Arms up . . . " Chris has them do that 4 more times.

After the last up and down, Chris says, "Relax. Close your eyes. Place the palms of your hands in your lap, on your legs, facing upwards, and just sit. Breathe in and out calmly naturally. Allow any thoughts your having to come and go. Just relax.

"Now, I want you to remember. See if you can picture the people I mention. Remember them. Remember what it was like in the moments I describe. Remember your *connections* with them.

"Remember George and the power of perspective, that no man or woman is an island. Remember your *connection* with George..

"Remember Abby the lioness and her dad—what a courageous leader and lover she is. Remember your *connection* with Abby.

"Remember Katya—saying 'I do' in baggage claim and how easily we can fall 'in-like' with each other. Remember your *connection* with Katya.

"Remember a great way to remember from the other Chris, his rubber-band and his aching wrist. Remember your *connection*.

"Remember Adrian, planting the seed and the 'Love *connection*. Remember your *connection*.

"Remember all the *extra*ordinary ordinary people just like you—and so very different from you—that you sat next to, shared with, laughed and cried with, applauded, appreciated, hugged heart-over-heart here today . . .

"Remember each other.

"Remember all the richly rewarding *connections* you experienced here today.

"Remember your *connection* to your God.

"CONNECT . . . OR DIE."

Chris pauses. "Open your eyes please." He takes a long time looking directly at as many faces as he can all through the audience. Then in a strong big voice he says . . .

"CONNECT . . . AND LIVE!"

"I love you," Chris says and walks off the stage.

ABOUT THE AUTHORS

Chris Dorrity

Davis Christopher Dorrity is a preacher, teacher, trainer, speaker and coach. Starting in 2007, Chris created the largest youth group in the nation. In his eclectic career he has played professional football, been a pro wrestler, restaurant owner, entrepreneur, and has been given the title "God's coach" by the numerous people he had counseled over the years. As an international speaker he's shared the stage with superstars such as John Maxwell, Tony Robbins and Gary Vanerchyk. He is the visionary leader of the "Connect Or Die" experience transformational weekend workshops and retreats.

Chris has been married to his childhood sweetheart, Sabrina—an award winning teacher—for 19 years and they have 3 "super-star" kids: Fifteen year old Reagan, already a star tennis player. Riley, who's 11 and an up and coming rock star singer. And Raney Hope, age 9, a budding business prodigy and star comedian. The Dorritys live in Macon ("You famous") Georgia.

John Milton Fogg

John Milton Fogg is a writer, editor, interview host, speaker and mentor-coach. He's written and edited over two-dozen books, and is the author of *The Greatest Networker in the World*, which has been read by more than 3 million people around the world. John has spoken internationally for more than 25 years in Iceland, India, and Iran, to Russia, Thailand and Taiwan. His life's work—and latest book—is *Speaking and Listening. We Don't Listen and We Talk Too Much*, which is being developed into an on-line course and coaching program.

John is the father of four children: Rachel, 37. Johnny 33. And as he says, "I had to make my own grandchildren," Ele, who's 16 and Anais, 12. He lives with his family in "Thomas Jefferson's Virginia."

www.ingramcontent.com/pod-product-compliance
Lightning Source LLC
Chambersburg PA
CBHW052036070526
44584CB00016B/2063